Arctic Convoy PQ-8

Arctic Convoy PQ-8

The Story of Captain Robert Brundle
and the SS *Harmatris*

by

Michael Wadsworth

Pen & Sword
MARITIME

First Published in Great Britain in 2009 by
Pen & Sword Maritime
an imprint of
Pen & Sword Books Ltd
47 Church Street, Barnsley, South Yorkshire S70 2AS

ISBN 978-1-84884-051-5

Typeset in 10/12pt Palatino by
Concept, Huddersfield

Printed and bound in England by
CPI UK

Pen & Sword Books Ltd incorporates the Imprints of Pen & Sword Aviation,
Pen & Sword Maritime, Pen & Sword Military, Wharncliffe Local History,
Pen & Sword Select, Pen & Sword Military Classics, Leo Cooper,
Remember When, Seaforth Publishing and Frontline Publishing.

For a complete list of Pen & Sword titles please contact
PEN & SWORD BOOKS LIMITED
47 Church Street, Barnsley, South Yorkshire, S70 2AS, England
E-mail: enquiries@pen-and-sword.co.uk
Website: www.pen-and-sword.co.uk

Contents

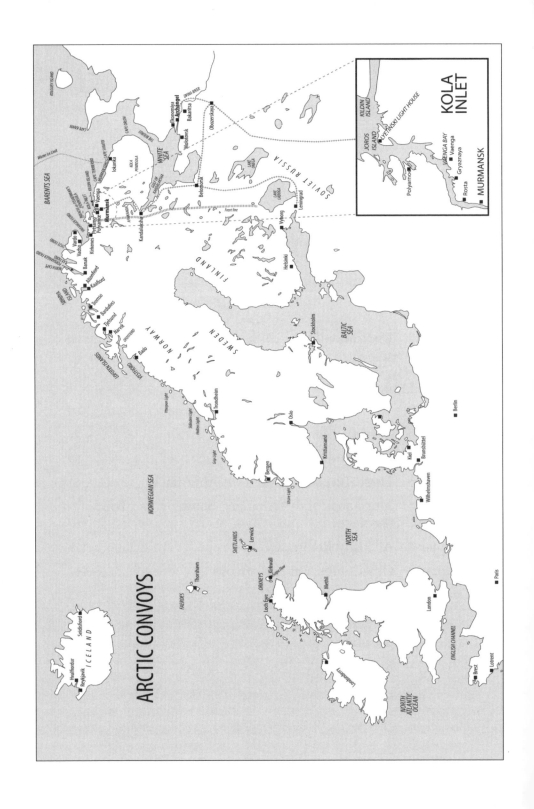

ARCTIC CONVOYS

KOLA INLET

MURMANSK

Dedication

This book is dedicated to Margaret Wadsworth and Eileen Hodgson, the daughters of Captain Robert Brundle, and to Richard, Paul and James Hodgson, who, with me, are his grandchildren.

Michael Wadsworth

'Look to the rock from which you are hewn'
(Isaiah 51:1)

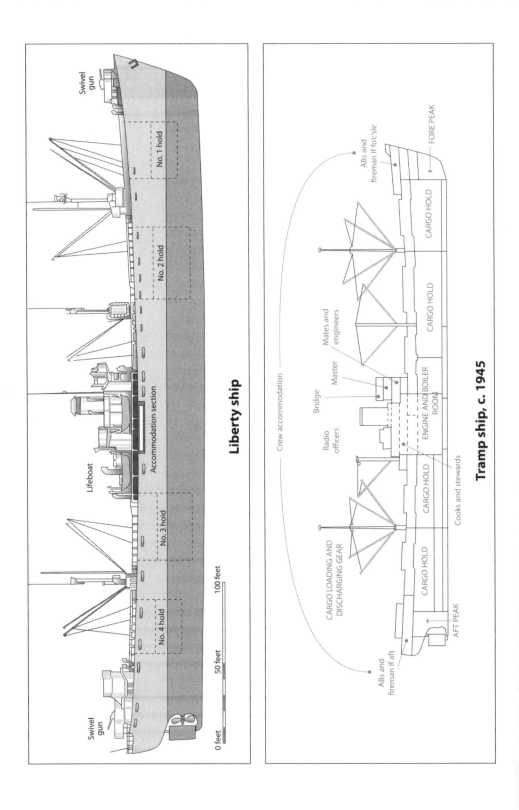

Liberty ship

Swivel gun

No. 1 hold

No. 2 hold

No. 3 hold

No. 4 hold

Accommodation section

Lifeboat

Swivel gun

0 feet   50 feet   100 feet

Tramp ship, c. 1945

Crew accommodation

ABs and fireman if fo'c'sle

FORE PEAK

CARGO HOLD

CARGO HOLD

Mates and engineers

Master

Bridge

Radio officers

ENGINE AND BOILER ROOM

CARGO HOLD

CARGO HOLD

Cooks and stewards

CARGO LOADING AND DISCHARGING GEAR

ABs and fireman if aft

AFT PEAK

Acknowledgements

Thanks are due to those who have helped me with advice and comments during the writing of this book: Adrian Carey, Frank Cheffings, Philip Jinks, Ken Pike, Winnie Sibley.

Special thanks are due to Richard Clash, of T.R. Clash Ltd, for his expertise with photographs, maps and diagrams, and for much sound technical advice; to Squadron Leader Andy Thomas for photographs of ships and aircraft on Russian convoys, for permission to use them, and for much advice and encouragement, out of his amazing fund of knowledge, along the way; to the Commercial photographic team of the Hull Daily Mail, Mail News and Media Ltd, and for their permission to reproduce a portrait of Captain Brundle printed in a wartime newspaper of March 1943; to Macmillan Publishers Ltd, through their literary agents, David Higham Associates Ltd, for their permission for me to quote a poem by the late Charles Causley, 'Song of the Dying Gunner AA1' from his Collected Poems 1951–1975 (p. 6), published by Macmillan in 1975; to the Trustees of the Imperial War Museum for permission to reproduce several of their excellent stock of photographs; to Anne Smillie-Pearson for typing the manuscript with conscientiousness and efficiency. Without her this book would not have seen the light of day; to my wife, Tamara Wadsworth, for her love, support and encouragement.

Michael Wadsworth

CHAPTER 1

A Garden Shed called Murmansk

I remember the black wharves and the slips
And the beauty and the mystery of the ships,
And the magic of the sea.
And the voice of that wayward song
Is singing and saying still:
'A boy's will is the world's will
And the thoughts of youth are long, long thoughts.'

Henry Wadsworth Longfellow,
'My Lost Youth', 1858

'Property of US Government'

As a boy I slept in sheets stamped 'Property of US Government'. At home my grandfather, who lived with us, would rise from his chair when he wanted to do a bit of gardening, and say 'I'm just going to Murmansk'. 'Murmansk' was the shed at the bottom of the garden. He used to go and sit on a cucumber frame in front of this shed, staring out into the middle distance at the cornfields of rural East Yorkshire. Clearly the shed was more than a shed and functioned as a trigger to recall memories.

Thereby hangs a tale. The story underlying both of these elements is that the sheets I slept in were taken from bombed and

1

partially sunken vessels in Murmansk harbour in 1942, where merchant seamen had to salvage and forage simply to stay alive, in a kind of 'Waste not, want not' spirit. In their foraging the seamen looked for food mainly, but also for the other necessities of life like sheets and bedding during the enforced months of waiting in the bombed-out port. Hence my American bed-linen, a deep wartime legacy.

'Murmansk', the name of my grandfather's garden shed, was a port on the Kola inlet of North Russia to which my grandfather brought his steamer, the SS *Harmatris*, with a cargo of ammunition, military vehicles, including tanks, machinery and provisions for the Soviet war effort in January 1942. Due to the drift ocean current in the North Atlantic, the ocean at this point is, as it were, warmed up, so that Murmansk remains ice-free all the year round, the only port in the region which is like this. In the Sami language of Russian Lapland 'Murmansk' means the 'edge of the world'.

Churchill's promises to Russia

When Germany invaded Russia in June 1941, most of her military equipment was destroyed in the first weeks of the invasion. On 1 October the first 'Moscow Protocol' was signed, whereby Britain and the USA (although not yet officially in the war) agreed to supply the USSR with war material and equipment. Churchill informed Stalin a few days later on 6 October, 'We intend to run a continuous cycle of convoys leaving every ten days'. In fact the first convoy, Operation Dervish – a kind of experimental convoy, had already sailed some time earlier, on 12 August, from Liverpool and had arrived in Archangel on 31 August.

Churchill's magnanimous decision left the Royal Navy, already preoccupied with the stresses of Atlantic convoys, Britain's own lifeline, impossibly overstretched. This cost, this expenditure of ships and men was well-nigh impossible. And yet, without the thousands of tons of weapons, machinery and materials provided by British, American and allied merchant seamen, it is doubtful whether the Red Army, for all their unique courage, could ever have held up the relentless German advance after the

June invasion. Before the USA joined the war, which she did after the Pearl Harbor attack on 7 December, while my grandfather was fighting a ship's fire during his abortive participation in convoy PQ-6, Britain was fighting alone, and so simply had to back Russia.

PQ-8 and my grandfather, Captain R.W. Brundle

This book attempts to explore the story behind the bed sheets, and the aptly named bleak-looking garden shed, and to use the story of convoy PQ-8 (as it was called) in December/January 1941/42, and the costly return journey of the SS *Harmatris* in late 1942 to illustrate the wider context of the Russian convoys and of the war in general. Outgoing convoys to Russia, please note, were named PQ- (and then 1, 2, 3, 4 etc) after the initials of Commander Philip Quellyn Roberts, a planning officer in the Admiralty, while homebound convoys were designated QP- (1, 2, 3 etc).

Because my father, Flying Officer Philip Wadsworth, had been killed in the Bomber Offensive, flying in the RAF Pathfinder Force, my grandfather was responsible for a lot of my early upbringing. After eventful service in two world wars, in the last war as Master of the SS *Harmatris*, he died in 1960 aged 66. Wartime strains had taken their toll. His name was Robert William Brundle (Bob Brundle to his friends and loved ones), and for the actions recounted in this book, in convoy PQ-8, he was awarded an OBE and the Lloyd's War Medal.

Among my principal sources are the documents from his reports (several had to be made to the Admiralty after he arrived back in convoy QP-14), his diaries and memorabilia, including newspaper cuttings. They give a unique, personal view by the Master of a British vessel (owned by J. & C. Harrison of London) of the progress of a troubled convoy, in which he was appointed Commodore, and of his eight months in Murmansk and Archangel, observing the lives and straitened circumstances of the inhabitants in the interludes between the bombings, and his struggle, using meagre and unpromising resources, to repair the ship, discover and distribute food among the crew, and, along with this crew, simply to stay alive and return home safe and sound.

Shape and pattern of the book

The book is in five parts:

1. The outward journey, comprising a false start with PQ-6, and then a journey to Murmansk, as Commodore of PQ-8 (chapters 1 to 5).
2. Eight months in Murmansk and Archangel (chapter 6).
3. The return journey, QP-14, September and October 1942. *Harmatris* and other merchant ships in the convoy had some survivors of PQ-17 on board, and the convoy was frequently under attack, with the sinking of some merchant ships and Royal Navy escort ships (chapter 7).
4. A survey of 'moments' in the long story of Russian convoys, which illuminate and set in perspective the character and promise of convoy PQ-8 (chapter 8).
5. Conclusions to be drawn. The life of Robert Brundle, including his being mined in Albanian waters in 1947. His premature death. 'Home is the Sailor' (chapter 9).

PQ-8: a watershed

Convoy PQ-8 was a watershed in the progress of the Russian convoy story. It was the first convoy to suffer significant casualties. On 17 January 1942, *U-454*, a German U-boat on the Arctic station, sank one of PQ-8's escorts, the Tribal Class destroyer HMS *Matabele*, north-east of the Kola Peninsula, with the loss of 209 persons. Only two were picked up alive.

In short, with air attacks, submarine attacks, and assaults by the weather, not to mention the ship's fire at the start, the story of PQ-8 is the story of the Russian convoys in microcosm, with the aftermath of eight weary months in Murmansk and Archangel providing an eloquent commentary on the plight of recipients of British aid in these desperate circumstances.

It is of no small interest that, although we are focusing in the main on PQ-8, this story tells of three convoys: PQ-6, PQ-8 and QP-14. *Harmatris* set off with PQ-6, but a horrendous Arctic storm slowed her down, and the discovery of the fire in her 'tweendecks did the rest, and she was forced to withdraw from the convoy and go back to Port Glasgow, there to wait for another convoy. It is interesting to speculate how different Brundle's adventures would have been, had he stayed and sailed with PQ-6. Two ships in the convoy were directed to Murmansk. The remainder, which might have included *Harmatris*, were assigned to the port of Molotovsk, on the White Sea, near Archangel.

Had that been the case, Brundle would have languished there, with the other five ships, locked in the ice until June, with a Russian icebreaker, which broke into the Gourlo channel, but could not break out again, and whose presence was utterly redundant, for all the difference it made to those five beleaguered ships of PQ-6.

Convoy history and procedure

Various adventures, various eventualities along the way of the story of *Harmatris* shed a light on convoy procedure and convoy history, and so Brundle had an encounter with the Naval Control of Shipping Officers (NCSO) in Rothesay Anchorage, and had to make a formal report on his early return from sailing with convoy PQ-6. He had to contact the owners, J. & C. Harrison in London.

Procedures like these are a fascinating gloss on the question of convoy discipline and on relations between owners and the management, as well as telling interested readers of Russian convoy literature just what happened, if you were constrained, for a very good reason, to drop out of a convoy.

From PQ-6 to PQ-8

The fire in *Harmatris* that was noticed and fought just after leaving Iceland changed the lives of her Master and crew in no small measure. Back in Port Glasgow, to which *Harmatris* had to return, it was most important for the damaged elements in the cargo of *Harmatris* to be renewed and replaced, as well as for the bulk of the cargo, which remained undamaged, to be checked and made secure, where necessary, a time-consuming process that took two weeks. The departure of *Harmatris* to join convoy PQ-8 on Boxing Day 1941 was the start of an adventure for Brundle and the crew which saw them through a momentous and eventful convoy. They were torpedoed three times off the Kola inlet, abandoned, re-boarded, were towed to port, attacked from the air, and yet they and *Harmatris* reached Russia. There then followed an eight-month struggle to repair the ship and so take their place in a return convoy. The damage included a hole 60 feet by 30 feet (18 metres by 9 metres), and much harm done to the upper structure of the ship, which resembled a pepper pot, and all this against a background of hunger and a continual battle to find food, first in Murmansk and secondly in Archangel.

To find food was the vital, overwhelming daily task; that and to protect ship and crew from the bombing. The return journey in QP-14 was a hazardous process, with multiple attacks and the loss of three escort ships and three merchantmen. So the tale of *Harmatris* is a story of highs and lows, of suffering and death, in which the theatre shifts from the stricken *Harmatris* outside the Kola inlet to the exploding *Matabele*, from two enemy aircraft spraying bullets over *Harmatris* and *Speedwell*, to *Harmatris* at her berth in Murmansk, reeling under the impact of multiple explosions from thrice-daily bombings.

As we ponder during this narrative Brundle's story, we shall learn many things. We will first look over the shoulder of a young boy from a very ordinary family, who was passionate about the sea, and committed to a life at sea, even though his father, himself a merchant seaman, was not keen on the idea, and did all that he could to put him off the call to the sea: 'No son of mine will go to sea', he said, with his fistful of memories of a hard life at sea. However, there must have been a sneaking pride in Robert William Brundle Senior, when his son gained one of the coveted scholarships to Hull Trinity House Navigation School, and whatever his reservations, he stood surety for him and signed his indentures when he was apprenticed to Captain Herbert Denholm Meek of SS *Riplingham*, owned by the East Riding Steamship Company of Goole.

The child is indeed father of the man. And so we go with him, Robert William Brundle Junior, now aged 47, on the journey that became the defining experience of his life, which undoubtedly hastened his end, but which for his family and for those who knew and loved him is written on the tables of our hearts.

N.B.
PQ-8 has been written about, together with the story of Captain Brundle and *Harmatris*, in Richard Woodman's *Arctic Convoys* (John Murray 1994), pp. 46–48 and pp. 56–58; in Bernard Edwards's *The Road to Russia* (Pen and Sword 2002), pp. 1–4 and 8, and *The Merchant Navy Goes to War* (Robert Hale 1990), pp. 77–87, and in David Wragg's *Sacrifice for Stalin* (Pen and Sword 2005) pp. 67–68.

CHAPTER 2

'My Merchant Navy'
(King George V)

'Oh, where are you going to, all you Big Steamers,
With England's own coal, up and down the salt seas?'
'We are going to fetch you your bread and your butter,
Your beef, pork, and mutton, eggs, apples, and cheese.'

'Then what can I do for you, all you Big Steamers,
Oh, what can I do for your comfort and good?'
'Send out your big warships to watch your big waters,
That no one may stop us from bringing you food.'

'For the bread that you eat and the biscuits you nibble,
The sweets that you suck and the joints that you carve,
They are brought to you daily by all us Big Steamers –
And if anyone hinders our coming you'll starve!'

Rudyard Kipling: 'Big Steamers' from
A History of England, 1911

Three Thousand Ships

The great and supreme target for German U-boats at the start of
the Second World War was the British merchant fleet. In those
days Britain boasted the largest merchant fleet in the world,
3,000 ships, with a 17-million-ton carrying capacity. Such a large

merchant fleet was needed because Britain needed to import over a third of her food and most of her raw materials (except for coal), 95 per cent of all petroleum products, 100 per cent of raw rubber, 80 per cent of soft timber, and 80 per cent of wool. It was a fragile supply line, intensely vulnerable to U-boat attack in time of war.

The leader of Hitler's U-boats, Admiral Dönitz, wanted a major expansion of his U-boat fleet to strike at Britain's merchant ships. He was keenly aware of lessons to be learned from the First World War, when Germany nearly brought Britain to her knees sinking 4,837 allied merchant ships, most in the period from 1917 onwards. It was the introduction of the convoy system by Lloyd George, the first of which, on 10 May 1917, began her voyage across the Atlantic, which largely stopped the appalling rate of sinkings.

Much blood, however, was spilt in the Second World War, in which the convoy system was taken for granted as a *modus operandi*. Thirty-five thousand merchant seamen, British and allied, perished, a higher death rate, in proportion to their numbers than that of any branch of the armed forces. Atlantic, Arctic and Malta convoys fed this rate of attrition. The total tonnage of allied shipping sunk in the Atlantic between July and September 1940 was 1,121,582, and, between October and December 1940, 1,034,930. Britain would effectively be starved if this were to continue.

The term 'Merchant Navy'

The term 'Merchant Navy' was what the press and propagandists called merchant ships and the seamen who manned them. No such thing really existed. 'Merchant Navy' was, in effect, a term or title of courtesy given to a big collection of ships owned by a heterogeneous group of companies, great and small, and the crews, who carried cargoes for profit along the world's seaways, whether these cargoes were basic heavy raw materials in quantity, or groups of passengers on stately, leisurely cruises. The ships ranged from coal-burning tramp steamers, the smaller of which gave off a lot of smoke under convoy conditions, to Cunard liners.

Ship-owners likewise ranged from the big boys: the Bank Line, Furness Withy, T. and J. Harrison of Liverpool, J. & C. Harrison of London, the Blue Funnel Line of Alfred Holt and the Ellerman Wilson Line of Hull, which, with their green hulls were known as the 'green parrots', to umpteen smaller companies in places like Cardiff, Hull, the Clyde, not to mention Goole, the end of the canal system, which Robert Brundle had sailed from as a young cadet in the early years of the twentieth century. The smaller companies paid their officers and ratings the minimum, and this was reflected equally in the quality of the food provided. The Merchant Navy, which always had its own brand of humour and a genius for naming things, called the smaller ships from such companies 'pound and pint' ships.

Holt and Harrison

Robert Brundle had experience of two of these bigger players, J. & C. Harrison of London, with whom he worked for thirty years, and Alfred Holt, originally of Liverpool, who designed and built their ships, carried their own insurance, and had an enlightened approach to the welfare of those they employed. J. & C. Harrison of London were a similar company, with high standards of ship maintenance and a benevolent approach to the needs and welfare of their employees. In the shipping industry of the 1920s and 1930s paid holidays were unheard of; but Holt and Harrison paid a retainer, which was much the same thing, appreciating the value of good seamen and able deck officers.

A memento of my grandfather's association with Alfred Holt was an ornamental wall plate, which had been taken from the SS *Telemachus*, and which hung in our house for years. Holt's, from the 1860s, when they operated as the Holt Brothers, had a penchant for Greek mythology (reflecting, no doubt, the family's Liverpool Unitarian tradition of plain living and high thinking, in which a classical education did not go amiss). They called their ships after Homeric gods and goddesses, and Greeks and Trojans. Inscribed at the bottom of the plate beneath a picture of the Olympian Immortals was a line from Homer's *Odyssey*, which can be translated as follows, though it seems a bit flat, or bland when taken out of context: 'And the very first to see her [Pallas Athene] was the godlike Telemachus.'

I was thrilled to be able to read and comprehend the original Homeric Hexameter. I could not come near my grandfather's quick mathematical wizardry, but he was thrilled that I could read the inscription on the plate. The inscription gave us a view of the Holt brothers of a hundred years before who had embarked on a classical education. Educational standards in those days were high for ship-owners, and high for Masters and officers, although it is unlikely that many of them would have been able to read Homer.

Indeed, the Holts regarded all their ships as embarking on some kind of Homeric Odyssey. The names of their ships reflected this, their distinctive livery, light blue with a black topped funnel reinforced this, and the company insisted on strength (a specially reinforced merchant hull) and seaworthiness in their products.

In the 1930s the Holt fleet was expanded when they purchased the Glen and Shire lines.

Now, whereas the merchant fleet of Great Britain amounted to about a third of the world's total tonnage, only about a quarter of all the tankers in the world were British. Major oil companies transported their own oil, with their own tanker fleets and their own specialised officers. It was left to Norway to rule the waves with her tanker fleet, and to benefit the allied side with this sudden access to tankers when Norway was occupied by the Germans. The plain fact of the matter is that, up to the second wartime emergency that brought Norwegian tankers to British shores, Norway invested in tankers, while Britain didn't.

Economic depression and the shipping industry

At the beginning of the war in 1939 the shipping industry was emerging from the long shadow cast by a great depression. The world's economic crisis had led to a collapse in the market for coal, and many vessels were laid up for want of a cargo.

When war broke out, therefore, the ships that had been laid up for want of cargoes were not able to put to sea for want of crews. A body called the Ministry of War Transport (MOWT) took over the work of providing ships and crews from the Board of Trade, but it was a struggle to provide all the men needed and to continue urgently promoting the training of cadets and apprentices to reach their standards of professional competence.

Seamen in peacetime 'signed up' for each voyage under 'Articles of Agreement', a contract which was terminated, and under which pay stopped, when a ship was sunk. Hence you could lose your life and your widow could lose the pay forthcoming to you at one and the same time.

This was an anomaly and an iniquity which was remedied after two years of wartime. A 'pool' of seamen, the Merchant Navy Pool, was created, continuously providing crews for ships, in April 1941, while in the next month the Essential Work Order compelled former seamen between the ages of 18 and 60 to reregister for sea duty. Under the regulations a seaman's pay continued until he was repatriated. Thus an early application to the Pool and a quick return to sea was actively encouraged.

The Naval Control of Shipping Officers

To keep the channels of communication at the ports in wartime alive and up to date, the work of the Admiralty was maintained, and concerns, great and small, were met and resolved by a body called The Naval Control of Shipping Officers (NCSO). Retired naval officers largely staffed this body. They handled the movement by ships in British and American ports, and very much took up the concerns of the ships' Masters, checking confidential books and code books, answering requisitions for equipment, seeing to it that emergency repairs were carried out, planning and organising the pre-convoy conference, and going from ship to ship when the convoy was assembling in harbour. The NCSO took careful note of the morale of merchant seamen, and were sympathetic to the needs and difficulties of the Masters and their ships.

Enter the free navies, Norwegian, Dutch and Greek

Britain acquired 233 tankers and well over 600 freighters and cargo vessels from the Norwegian mercantile marine. Churchill, in characteristic hyperbole, declared them 'worth a million soldiers'.

Norway, of course, had fallen to Hitler's forces on 7 June 1940, and King Haakon, Crown Prince Olav and the Norwegian government were rescued and transported to the UK by HMS *Devonshire*. The rich haul of shipping, including all those tankers, came about because the government in exile transmitted a vital radio message instructing all Norwegian merchant ships to sail for British ports. Norwegian merchant seamen, who, following instructions, placed themselves under British command, were well respected in our merchant service for their expertise, experience and knowhow. Dutch seamen, like the Norwegians, had a way with ships that, it was agreed, placed them head and shoulders above the rank and file. There were handfuls of Dutch and Norwegian seamen on several of the merchantmen in the convoys, as well as some ships, including the Norwegian tankers mentioned, entirely manned by their native crew.

The Dutch writer Jan de Hartog, who has been called the Joseph Conrad of the Netherlands, writes about these seamen in exile in his novel *The Captain*, which culminates in an account of a costly voyage to Murmansk.

But the Norwegians, it was felt in the seamen's own private world, had the edge over others. Their skill as seamen was honed and developed in the navigation of those broken and indented coastlines in their native land, as well as in service on board of deep sea trawlers in the Arctic fishing grounds, also near their native land. Whereas Britain pre-war had the largest merchant fleet in the world, its next three rivals, in size at any rate, were the USA, Japan and Norway (which ranked just above Germany), and the Norwegian fleet was growing all the time.

Wherever they went, in public houses, bars or cafes, the Norwegians were popular, not, on account of their spending power (like the Americans), but because of their exile status (Free Poles, Belgians, Greeks, Danes and Dutch were likewise so regarded), and because of their reputation as brilliant seamen. My grandfather once heard, in a Hull public house, 'Here come the Norwegians, boys. Here come the real sailors.' Their maritime pride and pedigree stretched back to embrace their Viking past. They were born with an instinct for navigation. There is one legend about a sextant being found in a Norwegian infant's pram. In the same way as Jan de Hartog lauded the

Dutch seamen in exile in his novels about the Second World War, so too the writings of Per Hansson, who once wrote for *Dagbladet*, Oslo's largest newspaper, do the same for Norwegian seamen. His novel *One in Ten Had to Die* is a vivid evocation of the lives of Norwegian sailors on Atlantic convoys. There are many references in it to the strains and trials of the Arctic convoys, and of the fearsome reputation the Murmansk run had for all those who sailed on it.

Also familiar in many an Arctic convoy was the sight of a Greek ship. When Greece was invaded in 1941 large numbers of Greek shipping made for British ports and, like the Norwegians and Dutch, augmented the British merchant fleet. There were also present in many convoys, both Atlantic and Arctic, chartered Panamanian ships, and other flag-of-convenience ships. Most of these were American-owned.

Most of the seamen from countries occupied by the Germans, sailing in British convoys, were not to see their families or their homeland again for five years. It is sad too to recall that, as they found themselves in the thick of the convoy struggle, taking part in all the major ones, not a few of these seamen from the occupied countries never returned to their homeland or saw their families again. They played a significant role, these seamen exiles, in the allied contribution to victory. Scattered among the crews of a variety of merchant ships, taken home on leave and 'adopted' by British crews and individuals within crews, they brought with them a kind of iron determination, which our own merchant seamen remembered and recounted with relish and affection.

The need for ships in wartime

But the British government, at this crucial time, at the very out-set of war needed to acquire in as short a time as possible the means to wage war. Britain was getting the ships, particularly the tankers, but she needed the raw materials, the very stuff of war, like bauxite and iron ore, and the means of steel production. Britain needed to charter more cargo-carriers, and needed the surge of vessels from the allied free navies of Europe. So she was compelled to enlist the help of neutral navies, like Sweden, who were prepared to run the risk of convoy, and those merchant fleets that flew a flag of convenience, Panama, Liberia and Honduras, even though the ghostly owners and managers could be traced back to the United States. Britain would get away her cargo by hook or by crook. She was fighting for her life, the life that came in on the convoys. Every bit of every cargo was vital, vital to Britain now, as it became vital to the USSR in times to come.

Royal Navy and Merchant Navy

This new influx of ships and men sharpened the allied merchant service and gave body and substance to the term 'Merchant Navy'. It was indeed, an official confirmation of a cosmopolitan status the Merchant Navy had, in a smaller measure, enjoyed even in peacetime. An element of old-fashioned snobbery and class distinction clung inevitably to the regard or lack of it a certain kind of RN officer had for their counterpart in the Merchant Marine, as the Merchant Navy's alternative, official name was. Between the Royal and Merchant Navies there was, as you can imagine, an element of competition. Some of it was friendly rivalry. Not all of it was good-natured.

The vicissitudes and stern necessities of war were to change all this. Inevitably the convoy experience, whether Atlantic, Arctic or Mediterranean, flung together both services, and most, if not all RN officers who came into contact with Merchant Navy personnel were impressed with their seamanship, hardihood and sheer guts in difficult situations. The officers commanding the destroyers, cruisers and minesweepers were particularly moved to comment on how the Masters of merchant vessels led their crews without benefit of and recourse to the Royal Navy Discipline Act, their leadership being embodied in their absolute strength of character. Merchant seamen were a class on their own, who eschewed the disciplinary code of the Senior Service, but who would follow a Master they trusted and respected to the ends of the earth, or even to Murmansk, for that is what the name means in the language of Russian Lapland.

Accompanying British and other allied European ships in any convoy were numbers of merchant vessels of the USA, both before and after Pearl Harbor. The shipyards of the USA were a success story all of their own, pioneering the building of ships that contained welded plates, which saved time and lent the building of these ships to mass production. Before America entered the war she had built 60 ships for Britain, cargo ships of the Ocean Class, while after full entry into the war the USA built 2,710 of the famous Liberty ships. A civil construction mogul from American industry, Henry J Kaiser, who had no previous experience in shipbuilding, headed up the very successful experiment in mass-producing these Liberty ships for the wartime emergency.

Liberty ships, Henry Kaiser and Thompson's of Sunderland

The prehistory of the Liberty ships, however, derives from the very pre-war depression that caused the shortage in shipping in the first place. Thompson's shipyard at Sunderland on the Wear sought to modernise their plant and facilities, as soon as they felt they could see light at the end of the tunnel after the great depression. One of the ships Thompson's built for Hall Brothers, a firm of Newcastle owners, the 10,000-ton vessel *Embassage*, was a bit of an ugly duckling, but a good, basic, hardwearing ship of pellucidly simple construction, so much so that the MOWT ordered the Thompson ships copied on both sides of the Atlantic.

Crippling losses in the Atlantic convoys demanded that the allies build and commission ships faster than the German U-boat could sink them, something which was not now happening. In this context, therefore, of extreme emergency, *Empire Liberty* (based on *Embassage*), that first Thompson ship, which was to be much copied by Henry Kaiser, was the ship which won this particular phase of the merchant vessel U-boat tonnage war.

All Kaiser's welded ships were called henceforth 'Liberty ships' after that first Thompson production, *Empire Liberty*.

Henry Kaiser in the USA created vast construction sites, eight new shipyards on the Atlantic coast, four on the Gulf of Mexico, and six on the Pacific coast. American Liberty ships were named after American heroes, *Patrick Henry, Paul Luckenbach,*

William S. Thayer. They were found in every convoy that sailed, in increasing numbers throughout this very long war.

Canada too copied the Liberty ships. Those named after 'Parks' were not only Canadian-built, but Canadian-crewed, while the ships that were Canadian-built and crewed by the British were named after 'Forts' – *Fort Bellingham*, *Fort Yukon* and the like. But the standard 'Thompson' ship was mass-produced in Britain as well. Cyril Thompson, son of the chairman of J.L. Thompson, went over to the USA to assist Henry Kaiser in the mass reproduction of his ship, then to Canada to continue this work, and back from Canada to Britain, where mass production continued. Such ships, based on the Thompson original, but built in Britain, had 'Empire' prefixed to their names. Hence *Empire Starlight*, *Empire Tourist*, *Empire Ranger*, and so on. Captured enemy ships were also often given the prefix *Empire*. Some of these Thompson's Liberty standard ships, with their good basic design, had a use as a ship with a specialist application. And so *Empire Morn* and *Empire Tide* were CAM (Catapult Aircraft Merchant) ships, catapulting Sea Hurricanes to meet the challenge of enemy fighters attacking the convoys, while *Empire Bard*, the well-named *Empire Buttress* and *Empire Elgar* were heavy-lift ships, which, until they were constructed, were seriously lacking, particularly among the wharfs and berths of Murmansk. This co-operation between a small Sunderland shipbuilder and the American mogul Henry Kaiser was one of the ineluctable ingredients of victory in the convoy war.

The celebrated British broadcaster and commentator Alistair Cooke, who delivered his famous 'Letter from America' on British radio, spoke of how he visited Kaiser's Richmond shipyard in California, which seemed to him like a kind of perpetual motion machine, with 30,000 components whizzing this way and that. Those assembling all the parts, Cooke averred, knew less about building ships than the boss and managing director, Henry Kaiser, who took delight in confounding the specialists, especially when they said something couldn't be done, that such and such a thing was impossible.

President Roosevelt commented on the ships as 'dreadful-looking objects'. To add to the unsightliness they had a strong, competitive armament, a 4-inch low-angle surface defence gun, and an AA system made up of a 12-pounder, 40mm Bofors and 20mm Oerlikon guns, as well as Parachute And Cable (PAC) rockets. And they made a comfortable 11 knots, 3 knots more than the normal 8 knots of the standard, plodding convoy. Kaiser talked about the 'front' and 'back' end of a ship, and the specialists in shipbuilding scoffed at him. 'I don't care what he calls them, provided he delivers', Roosevelt said in his defence.

These 'ugly' ships had a uniquely successful history. Apart from their obvious and decisive usefulness in the Arctic and Atlantic campaigns they formed the focus of the world's post-war merchant fleet. You saw them everywhere, sailing everywhere. When someone in post-war shipping circles made a reference to a 'Liberty-size cargo', he meant a standard bulk shipment of 10,000 tons. The phrase took on a life of its own. It became a standard unit in the chartering companies.

Many Liberty ships, therefore, had long and productive careers after the war. It was the Liberty ship, with the converted C-type hull, which was to serve as the first experimental container ship. War and the demands of war provide the great catalyst for changes and alterations in design and function.

American seamen: the need for trained officers

But construction, successful and speedy, was only one part of the problem. The other side of the problem was that there was a shortage of trained men, especially from the American mercantile marine. There was a poverty of merchant seamen to cope with this wartime expansion of merchant shipping; a greater number of ships, but no crews to man them.

To solve this problem America, in typical 'can-do' spirit, set up three large training establishments to create and equip new merchant seamen with the skills they needed, one on the eastern seaboard at Sheepshead Bay, Brooklyn, one on the Great Lakes at Waukegan, Illinois, and the third on the Pacific west coast at Treasure Island, San Francisco. There were also government training schools for officers, and – something which caused friction off duty in ports – an American Able Seaman was paid, on average, almost double the wages of his British counterpart. Methods of American mass production of ships and seamen alike were derided by British seamen. Nevertheless the added increase of American ships on the Atlantic convoys, and crews to sail in them, quite literally saved Britain from starvation.

In PQ-8, my grandfather's convoy to Murmansk, there was present an American freighter, *Larranga*, which was vice commodore, after my grandfather's commodore ship, *Harmatris*.

Officers in the Merchant Navy

There was never a shortage of cadets and apprentices being trained to take their place as officers in the Merchant Navy. There were three officers (sometimes four), First, Second and Third Officer under the Master, three Radio Officers, four Engineer Officers, including the Chief Engineer, or 'Chief'. There were also one or two apprentices or cadets in many seafaring ships in wartime. The cadet/midshipman was responsible for navigation, the loading and discharge of cargo, as well as the maintenance of hull, superstructure, cargo-handling equipment, and safety equipment, quite a responsibility for a boy in his mid-teens. And yet he had three officers, under the Master, keeping an eye on him, and the able seamen, who were responsible for carrying out maintenance work under the supervision of the Bosun, the senior rating, to carry out the work needed. Everybody slotted into place. Lastly there was the Steward, or the Chief Steward, in overall charge of catering, with cooks working to his orders, and of bed-linen, cleaning of officers' accommodation, and so on.

Boys who applied to join this hectic and dangerous life in wartime as cadet or apprentice had a family seafaring tradition, and needed to attend one of several navigation or seamanship schools dotted about the country in the main maritime ports. London, Hull, Glasgow, Southampton, Liverpool, Middlesbrough and Cardiff were the main ones. Boys went to sea in their mid-teens, as a cadet or an apprentice on a vessel, under strict indentures paid to the ship's owners by their family. As befits a nation with a seafaring tradition like Great Britain (and it must be emphasised that the Royal Navy emerged from the nation's mercantile traditions), some of these navigation schools were founded in the seventeenth or eighteenth centuries.

Cadets and apprentices: nurture and training

The training of cadets for the merchant marine was a requirement that had expanded with the needs of war. To keep pace with demand, there were other agencies of training apart from the celebrated navigation schools. Thus there were such training establishments as HMS *Conway* on the Mersey, little more than a redundant man-of-war, *Worcester* on the Thames, *Indefatigable* near *Conway* and the Gravesend Sea School. There was also, at the other end of the scale, the naval college at Pangbourne in Berkshire, which was of public school status. Those who attended these establishments, whether in peacetime or wartime were, it goes without saying, highly motivated, keen as mustard. They were conscious also, especially those who trained in the inter-war years or well into the twentieth century, of something like a Merchant Navy developing out there, something over and above the obligation of service to the owner of a vessel, and then the depression came and altered things for ever. It was left to the demands of war to sharpen and heighten the ambition towards service at sea.

Robert Brundle, the Hull Trinity House boy

My grandfather, Robert William Brundle Junior, to distinguish him from his father, Robert William Brundle Senior, was born and lived in 7 Arthur Grove, Manchester Street, Hull, the eldest of four children, and won a scholarship to the Hull Trinity House Navigation School during the closing years of the nineteenth century. The Hull Trinity House Marine School, as it was called upon its foundation, opened on 2 February 1787, with only thirty-six pupils, with the Curate of the nearby Sculcoates Church being the 'Master' (that is Headmaster). During my grandfather's time at the school the Headmaster was Mr Zebedee Scaping (a good Victorian, Dickensian-style name for a Dickensian-type character) who wrote that the school uniform consisted of 'a dress coat of blue cloth with long tails, lined with white, a stand up collar of white cloth and brass buttons, a blue waistcoat with brass buttons, and trousers of white duck or blue cloth'. Every boy wore a blue cloth cap of the Royal Naval pattern, which, for boys, must have been an improvement on the tall beaver hats they had to wear until 1854.

Thus clad and representing the honourable traditions of the Hull Trinity House Corporation, these diminutive sailors, seamen in miniature, seen around the streets of Hull, were marked men. They certainly knew where they were going, and they were set on a course which would bring this about.

The life at Trinity House was steeped in tradition for every boy attending. There was Founders Day or Dinner Day, when, as part of the celebrations, the boys were given a nice dinner, after which every boy was invited to take two oranges from a basket on a table behind him. This custom was said to have been introduced to prevent boys deliberately picking the large fruit. Manners were important at Hull Trinity House. So was religion. The boys were prepared for Confirmation by the clergy of Holy Trinity Church. The eighteenth-century foundation had a certain view of what they wanted a ship's Master to be. Manners (certainly) maketh man.

At the time of Hull Trinity House's foundation towards the end of the eighteenth century Hull was a thriving port. The slaving ships used to call there, which so pricked the conscience of the redoubtable William Wilberforce and made him begin the fight to abolish that 'odious traffic in human flesh'. The port's commercial prosperity and involvement with the maritime industry led to the foundation of the Hull Trinity House Marine School. In 1719, sixty-eight years before the school's foundation, Daniel Defoe's *Robinson Crusoe* was written, in which its eponymous character sets out from the city of Hull on the voyage that is to change his life, testimony surely to the city's popularity with seafarers, real as well as fictional. The boys of Hull Trinity House were following illustrious predecessors. They had the call of the sea ringing in their ears.

Robert Brundle signs his indentures

On 23 November 1909 Robert William Brundle Junior signed his indentures, when he was 15. He was apprenticed to a ship's Master, Captain Herbert Denholm Meek of the SS *Riplingham*. The vessel had been a part of the East Riding Steamship Company, owned by Herbert A. Meek and Sons of Goole. His father had to sign to stand surety for him. He was a merchant seaman too, a Coal Trimmer (as he indicates on the document of the indentures), that is someone in the engine-room who supplied coal to the firemen who stoked the fires.

The East Riding Steamship Company

The East Riding Steamship Company, from which came Robert Brundle's first ship, the SS *Riplingham*, was based in and operated from Goole. Indeed, Goole was, in those days – the first decade of the twentieth century – a thriving haven for shipping, and several ship-owners, with a number of vessels, used Goole as their port. Run by a Goole ship-owning family, the Meeks, the East Riding Steamship Company had seven steamers. *Riplingham's* Master was a member of the Meek family, Captain Herbert Denholm Meek. All the ships of the company ended in '-ingham'. Hence *Brantingham, Riplingham, Everingham, Otteringham, Cottingham, Winteringham, Keyingham*. The names are local place names in the Goole, Hull and Humber area. What was real was local in those days, and what was local was real, especially to someone contemplating a voyage on the high seas, and above all to someone who was only 15 years old, and who had the world, outside the broad Humber estuary, at his feet.

A four-year apprenticeship

The apprenticeship ran for four years. The apprentice was suitably admonished:

> *not to frequent alehouses or taverns ... Nor [to] play at unlawful games, in consideration whereby the said Master ... will and shall use all proper means to teach the said Apprentice, or cause him to be taught the business of a seaman, and the Master also agrees to provide the said Apprentice with sufficient meat, drink, lodging, medicine and medical and surgical assistance, and pay to the said Apprentice the sum of £30, in manner following; (that is to say) five pounds for the first year, six pounds for the second*

year, eight pounds for the third year, and eleven pounds for the fourth and last year, together with twelve shillings in each year in lieu of washing.

It was a tough life for the young Brundle in the Goole steamer. Senior cadets made him ingest pork fat as a means of surmounting and curing his incipient seasickness. Ships such as the SS *Riplingham* operated whenever and wherever there was a cargo to deliver or to fetch, from grain to bauxite, from timber and coal to iron ore. Such free enterprise, tramp steamers going for cargoes all over the world, was the rich foundation of Britain's commercial greatness in Edwardian times.

A Yorkshireman from Hull, Robert Brundle was a quick learner, stubborn and determined. He became a Master at the age of 29. At the age of 23, when he held his Chief Officer's 'ticket' (as the certificate was called) he married Annie Minns of Driffield in East Yorkshire. They had two children, Margaret (my mother) and Eileen.

For thirty years from 1918 to 1948 Robert Brundle worked for the company, J. & C. Harrison of London, formerly the Willis Steamship Company, sailing to every large port of the world. The names of range of ships J. & C. Harrison owned all began with the letters 'Ha'. Thus *Harpagus*, *Harpalion*, *Harmatris* and *Hartlebury*, to name but a few. When he took the SS *Harmatris* to Russia, Robert Brundle was 47 years old.

CHAPTER 3

Over the Top of the World

I tell you nought for your comfort,
Yea nought for your desire,
Save that the sky grows darker yet
And the sea rises higher.

G.K. Chesterton (1911)

I cannot forecast to you the action of Russia. It is a riddle
wrapped in a mystery inside an enigma.

W.S. Churchill, 1939

If Hitler invaded hell, I would make at least a favourable
reference to the devil in the House of Commons.

W.S. Churchill, 1941

Germany invades Russia: total collapse of the Stavka

Germany invaded Russia on 22 June 1941. For all the warning messages delivered by intelligence sources to the USSR, Stalin and the Soviet authorities were taken by surprise. The blow, when it fell, was almost crushing. By the end of the first day of invasion 1,500 Soviet aircraft had been destroyed on the ground and 322 shot down. Three Russian divisions were unaccounted for.

Stalin created a new Command structure. Old front-line commanders were shot in the grim Soviet and Stalinist manner, and Stalin, recovering from a mental breakdown, broadcast a rallying cry of defiance to the nation. On Sunday evening 22 June it was Churchill's turn to broadcast to the British nation. He pledged all possible assistance to the Russians against the common enemy.

In view of the future experience of the allied seamen who had manned the ships which sailed in convoy to Russia, it must be stated that the wartime alliance between Britain and the USSR was not like that between Britain and the USA. It was not a union of two states of the same mind and temper and ideology. The attitude of the Soviet Union towards Britain in June 1941 was, at best, one of distrust. They were united by the common aim of defeating Germany, 'making an alliance with the devil himself, in order to defeat Hitler', as Churchill, with his deep gift for words, put it. And yet Hitler's invasion of the USSR had transformed the strategic situation at a stroke. The British had been fighting against Hitler, with their backs to the wall. The great priority in this new situation, as Churchill saw it, was for Russia to be kept fighting, and for Russia to be kept fighting against Hitler.

Britain and America respond

It was a time for meetings, consultations, the sending of envoys. Stalin, of course, asked for the moon, or rather demanded the moon. He urged Britain and the USA to divert to Russia impossible quantities of supplies, and clamoured for the opening of a second front in Europe, equally impossible, a theme which, pipe dream though it was, awoke nascent members of the British Communist Party into plastering their graffiti all over Britain.

On 10 July Churchill proposed to dispatch a Royal Navy task force to consult with the Russians over the provision of material military aid. On 12 July an Anglo–Soviet agreement was signed that pledged mutual assistance between Britain and the USSR in the fight against Hitler, with no separate peace ever to be concluded between Stalin and Hitler. Admiral Philip Vian and Rear Admiral George Miles, therefore, went with a British military mission to Moscow, and from there visited some of the North Russian ports, Polyarnoe and Archangel. Vian and Miles, on their Russian journey, met Admiral Arsenii Golovko, Commander in Chief of the Northern Fleet, the pivotal figure in the future for all the dealings of the British with the Russians.

Back in Britain Vian briefed Admiral of the Fleet, Sir Dudley Pound, the First Sea Lord, and other chiefs of the services in a typically forthright, but negative way. He argued that there was no future in sending a task force to the Arctic, with 'twenty-four hours of daylight in the summer months', and with the Germans operating their U-boats, and 'airfields within thirty miles'.

The Chiefs of Staff accepted this view, only to be railroaded into something more than sending 'a submarine or two' by a promise given by Anthony Eden to the Soviet Ambassador in London, Ivan Maisky, that a naval force would be sent.

The meeting in Placentia Bay

After a tentative exploration of Spitzbergen as a place for the establishment of a base for naval operations, which proved totally unfit for the purpose, a meeting, a historic meeting, was held between Churchill and President Roosevelt, even though the USA was officially still a neutral power, at Placentia Bay in Newfoundland on board the battleship HMS *Prince of Wales*, a ship doomed in the forthcoming Japanese offensive early the following year. The meeting was a secret one, and HMS *Prince of Wales* crossed the Atlantic to rendezvous with the USS *Augusta* in Placentia Bay, Newfoundland on 9 August 1941. This was the first face-to-face meeting between Churchill and Roosevelt and thus was a momentous event. Roosevelt's personal envoy to Stalin, Harry Hopkins, had just returned from Moscow, and, after his report, aid was promised to the USSR on a gigantic scale.

Lord Beaverbrook, representing Britain, and Averell Harriman, representing the USA, headed a joint Anglo–American military mission to Russia, which emerged directly from this meeting at Placentia Bay. A joint declaration of intent was cemented, and American industrial military production was increased. The tentative initiatives set for this year of 1941, since the German invasion of Russia, may have boosted morale, but they did not directly help Russia in the current crisis into which she had been plunged.

What Russia needed was supplies. Men and materials had both been swept away by the swift and punitive and astonishing advance of the Germans into Russia in June. The German invasion had left a depleted Red Army with little to fight with. Meanwhile, Soviet military industries were being evacuated to the Urals. It was all being done on such a colossal scale, and the pledge of aid to Russia had to play its part alongside all of these processes. It was to be done on a grand scale too. A 'shopping list' was handed over by Stalin to Beaverbrook and Harriman. It consisted of vehicles, guns, aluminium for aircraft manufacture, and significantly, anti-aircraft (AA) guns.

Meanwhile, while these promises and pledges were being given and were being prepared for implementation, the Nazi invaders were pushing their initiatives home in two crucial areas. They had captured Novgorod and had laid siege to Leningrad on 4 September, while, on 19 October with von Bock and his panzers at the gates of Moscow, only 20 miles from Red Square, Stalin issued his Order of the Day: 'Moscow will be defended to the last.'

British wartime propaganda played its part when recourse was made to stimulating Britain's industrial military production. Churchill's gesture towards Russia was thought by service chiefs, cabinet members and others to be difficult to carry out. Ordinary folk, however, were, despite the 'Great Terror' and the liquidation of the kulaks, very well disposed towards 'Uncle Joe' Stalin. There was a 'Tanks for Russia' week on 22 September 1941. Where labour relations in one factory or another were less than smooth, you could ensure the speedy implementation of an order if you labelled it 'Goods for Russia'. At Ashford in Kent 1,000 railway wagons for Russia were completed in ten days despite 76 air-raid warnings. Robert Brundle's cargo in PQ-8 included railway wagons. They were vital equipment for the Russians at this particular time. Once again, what the Russians needed could only be brought to them by merchant ships, suitably escorted, with a big carrying capacity. *Harmatris*, Brundle's ship, had a carrying capacity of 8,000 tons. Most other merchant ships in a convoy had a similar capacity.

Convoys to North Russia

The atrocious weather made the story of the Russian convoys legendary, as did the hazards they faced all along the long route. The air was completely dominated by the Luftwaffe, while the Kriegsmarine, the German Navy ('our little Navy', as Hitler called it, obsessed as he was by the size of the Royal Navy), had some heavy ships in the fiords of Norwegian waters, since Hitler regarded the polar coast along which the convoys passed as a 'decisive area'. U-boats likewise had taken up station in these Arctic waters. Threats to the convoys were coming in from all sides.

The route of the Russian convoys was 1,500 miles from Iceland or 2,000 miles approximately from Great Britain. From Iceland the route ran by sea to the north Norwegian coast, and ultimately from the North Cape to the Kola inlet and Murmansk. The duration of this journey was from fifteen to seventeen days.

Royal Naval escorts: cruisers

Admiral Tovey stated that prudent strategy demanded that the Royal Navy set aside four cruisers, and eight destroyers, at the absolute minimum, for the work of escorting the convoys to North Russia.

Cruisers in the Second World War were usually deployed with a major fleet, or in supporting a convoy. HMS *Edinburgh* and HMS *Trinidad* were cruisers that were sunk on convoy escort duty, both on the Russian run. HMS *Scylla*, another cruiser that we shall encounter in our narrative, with her 4.5-inch guns, was known as 'the toothless tiger'. County Class cruisers had large hulls, strongly built to absorb punishment. They lacked some of the armament they needed for duels with the opposing fleet or for convoy protection in this long, hard war, but had high endurance and good sea-keeping qualities, which made them good ships to have around as escorts on gruelling Arctic convoys.

Royal Naval escorts: Flower Class corvettes

The building of what came to be known as the Flower Class corvettes, from a form and shape derived from an old whaling boat, but with triple expansion steam engines fed by Scotch boilers, was a godsend to anti-submarine warfare. They had an endurance rate of 4,000 miles, and their speed ranged from 10 to 16 knots. The significant drawback was that in heavy Atlantic or Arctic seas they rolled and pitched horribly. Until later modifications crept in, like the extension of the forecastle, the so-called 'Castle' Class, a corvette's crew got perpetually wet. The Flower Class was, in the raw actuality of the cruel sea, the antithesis of its collection of fragrant, land-based flower names, like *Verbena, Carnation, Celandine, Lotus, Poppy*, and the Free French *La Malouine*.

The Flower Class corvettes fulfilled the great need the Navy had for an effective and vital anti-submarine ship. Their genesis, as has already been explained, lay in the whaling ships that plied their trade in the Antarctic, oil-fired whale-catchers powered by steam, capable of being built and assembled and commissioned in large numbers. The corvette provided an escort and anti-submarine ship for the Royal Navy that could be accommodated within the demands of small merchant ship construction. The blueprint for design and construction was a whale-catcher, *Southern Pride*, the product of Smith's Dock Company of Middlesbrough on the Tees. It was good in submarine pursuit with a small hull, and, though it rolled and yawed, as has been said, it had a good range and endurance. Indeed, it was a popular and ubiquitous ship, for all its perceived shortcomings, and many 'hostilities-only' seamen cut their teeth on corvettes.

It was much loved by our gallant allies the 'free navies' of occupied Europe. The Greeks had four corvettes entirely manned by themselves, the Royal Yugoslavian Navy had another, the Dutch had one, and not to be left out, the Free French manned the corvette *La Malouine*, striking their tricolour on this vessel with great pride. When longer, improved hulls gave rise to the Castle Class of corvette, with yet more effective anti-submarine armaments, you had a first-class warship, capable of being procured rapidly, one which would go anywhere. The corvette helped to turn the tide in the Battle of the Atlantic, and played a significant part in the Arctic convoys too.

Halcyon Class minesweepers

The same was true of the Royal Navy's Halcyon Class mine-sweepers, which were longer and faster than the Flower Class corvettes. The 6th Minesweeping Flotilla, based at the Kola inlet, on the approaches to Murmansk, provided a local eastern escort for the PQ- ships coming in from Loch Ewe and Iceland. HMS *Harrier*, *Speedwell*, *Sharpshooter* and *Hazard* worked tirelessly to sweep the channels in the path of the incoming convoy vessels, and also to provide close escort when needed. *Speedwell* towed Brundle in the badly damaged *Harmatris* through air attack into Murmansk harbour. After a night and a day of embarking on *Speedwell* and disembarking, and afterwards being towed by *Speedwell* to Murmansk, relations between the merchant crew of *Harmatris* and the RN crew of the minesweeper were very close indeed, and boded well for relations between the two services.

An old friend of the convoys, one of these indefatigable mine-sweepers, HMS *Gossamer*, was sunk by Stukas in the Kola inlet in June 1942, while, in convoy QP-14 Brundle witnessed the sinking of another minesweeper, HMS *Leda*.

Royal Naval escorts: destroyers

Destroyers were seen much in evidence acting as escorts of the merchant ships in convoys. Dedicated to capital ships' protection, they had become fleet destroyers, especially in the heavily escorted convoys of the second part of the war. But we shall see them functioning often as devastating carriers and deliverers of torpedoes.

Tribal Class destroyers

Alongside the corvettes the Tribal Class destroyer, launched in the late 1930s and throughout the war, was another fast and lethal warship, providing an anti-torpedo deterrent amidst a battle fleet. Many of the Tribal Class destroyers were sunk during the long war, thirteen of a total complement of twenty-two. Brundle witnessed the sinking of both *Matabele* in convoy PQ-8, and *Somali* in QP-14. They were used extensively in convoy protection, especially in the Arctic convoys and they had a tough, hard war.

It has been said that the Tribal Class destroyers did not make hardy and durable long-range escorts for convoys. While not being exactly suitable for this purpose in their planning and inception, they assuredly played a memorable part in the defence of the convoy in the case of PQ-8, with *Matabele* making the supreme sacrifice, and *Somali* suffering casualties in QP-14. Indeed, their contribution throughout the war was exemplary. They were always there, in a tight corner, when the U-boats were at their most dangerous.

Hunt Class destroyers

The Hunt Class destroyers, which came on stream at the time the convoys were being sailed, were a faster escort ship and were equipped with a potent AA armament, invaluable in air attack. Like their sister Tribal Class destroyers, they were often in the thick of the action proving their mettle abundantly.

The Hunt Class destroyers were not as fast as the sleeker fleet destroyers; but, at 26 knots, they were faster than frigates, and found themselves frequently guarding and shepherding a convoy.

Town Class destroyers

Other destroyers frequently found on convoy work were the Town Class escort destroyers. They were old Lend-Lease ships, loaned to Britain by the US government, as were the Colony class. Both had a tough war. *Sheffield* and *Jamaica* were both involved in the battle of the Barents Sea in late 1942, and *Belfast* took part in the sinking of *Scharnhorst*, another Arctic action.

Indeed, you could say that the term 'destroyer' was almost a courtesy title among the *mélange* of vessels. Some destroyers were reclassified as frigates, of which there were thirty-one Loch Class built between 1943 and 1945. Often a convoy's 'destroyer' screen consisted of frigates, corvettes and minesweepers, and yet all of them, in their various ways, sought to complement one another and protect the convoy 'on its lawful occasion'.

Variety of escorts

There were other kinds of ship used as escorts by the Royal Navy. We shall see the introduction of a carrier, HMS *Avenger*, in convoy QP-14, something which became commonplace thereafter, in pace with the large and numerous escorts of PQ-18, QP-14 and onwards. And yet from the earliest convoys onwards the standard ships in an escort force, small or large, were cruisers, Tribal- (or Hunt-) Class destroyers, Flower Class corvettes, and minesweepers.

Indeed, the obligation to Russia stretched the resources of the Royal Navy to an almost impossible extent. The Navy, for their part, had never enough escorts, and were compelled to utilise every resource, from the fifty old Lend-Lease destroyers loaned to Britain before America entered the war to the old 'Woolworths' aircraft carriers, as they were affectionately known, and from Armed Merchant Cruisers to His Majesty's Trawlers. To meet these challenges mature and experienced seamen were needed all the time on every kind of vessel. As my grandfather used to say, 'seamen like this are born, not made.' That was, if anything, a self-referring remark, although he did not use it of himself, and would never say anything like this of himself. He enjoyed being commended for his efforts, and as he put it, 'for services rendered', while at the same time presenting a veneer of embarrassment about the whole thing. Pride and humility are really no distance apart. They go together.

And then there were other factors in the anti-U-boat offensive, which tipped the balance in the war the Russian convoys fought. To maximise and increase the AA capability of the Hunt and Tribal Class destroyers, AA auxiliary cruisers, specialist cruisers like *Pozarica* and *Palomares* were introduced, derived from the celebrated and well-loved McAndrew's fruit carriers. It really was a case of from banana boat to AA ship. They, and others like them, certainly made a difference to convoy protection. *Pozarica* and *Palomares* were among the densely packed escorts of QP-14, which included *Harmatris* among its complement of merchant ships.

Bletchley Park and Enigma

Yet another factor that caused the enemy discomfort was the deployment of efficient and workable Asdic sets throughout the escort fleet, which was of the utmost importance in the defeat of the U-boats. And the icing on the cake? This must be the intelligence derived from the wizardry and sheer brain power of those who worked at Bletchley Park. They may have been out of the front line in the conventional physical sense, but their unremitting attention to the seeking of decrypting solutions, as soon as the daily German signals had been broadcast and distributed, even at the cost of their own mental health, produced not a few casualties. For inevitably there were several breakdowns, as an unpleasant bi-product of such intense, pressured labour, as Robert Harris's popular novel *Enigma*, and the film derived from it, makes clear.

'Shark': blackout and breakthrough

For one lengthy period of 1942 (from February to December) the Admiralty's Operational Intelligence Centre was not in receipt of the flood of decryptions from Bletchley they had been used to. The Germans were using what they called 'Triton' and what we called 'Shark' on their Enigma machine, thereby imposing a code blackout, an intelligence hiatus which meant that in the Barents Sea and around the Kola inlet ships of a convoy could not (as was usual) be diverted away from the path of U-boat wolfpacks. The breakthrough in finding the key to Shark occurred in December 1942, thanks to the Germans using three-wheel rather than four-wheel settings for the transmission of short signals like weather reports. It was then relatively simple to work out the setting of the fourth wheel and hence to decode the Shark transmission.

The casualties of the Shark blackout were, among others, those who perished in convoy PQ-17, as well as those in the tragic consequences where individual ships were sunk in other convoys. I have encountered a number of those who worked at

Bletchley Park in recent years, and found them a modest and self-deprecating group of gifted individuals. Their tireless labour and devotion and use of their soaring intellects undoubtedly saved the lives of many, many allied seamen. To these 'Cinderellas' of the allied cause a considerable debt of gratitude is owed. Churchill knew this, the War Cabinet knew this, and the allied Chiefs of Staff knew this.

Convoys: the Coal-Scuttle Brigade

Meanwhile, the oceans were being crisscrossed with convoys. They were the small convoys of the so-called 'Coal-Scuttle Brigade', travelling from London, the Thames and the South-East to Methil on the Firth of Forth and other east-coast ports transporting coal to smaller bunkering ports. For Brundle there were many short-lived home runs like this, in between the longer and more fraught Atlantic and Arctic convoys.

Convoys: Atlantic and Mediterranean

A vast system of imports flowing from Freetown, Sierra Leone; from Kingstown, Jamaica; from Halifax, Nova Scotia; from the Suez Canal and Gibraltar, bestrode the convoy routes. Convoy codings reflected this: the prefix 'HX' denoted a convoy from Halifax to Britain, 'ONS' Outward North Slow between Britain and North America, 'ON' meant outward North from Liverpool, the Clyde and Northern Ireland towards North America. The 'SC' convoys, running from Sydney, Cape Breton Island to Britain, relieved the congestion in the Bedford Basin at Halifax, Nova Scotia. An alternative North American port was needed for slower vessels, to relieve congestion. In the winter months Sydney could not be used because of the loose pack ice.

There was hardly any relief for seamen between convoys: a short home run up E-boat alley or up to the Firth of Forth on the east coast was fraught with hazards. Men lost their lives through torpedoes, bomb and air attack on these short runs as much as on the celebrated Atlantic and Arctic. There were no rest cures, no milk runs. It was not rest and recuperation. Home runs demanded vigilance of a sharp and sustained nature. Not to be vigilant was to court death in one of its most unpleasant forms, coughing your heart out in an oil slick or trapped in a jammed and sinking engine-room. The convoy war imposed its own relentless pressure. Feeding a lifeline to a beleaguered Britain, or, from mid-1941, to a Soviet Union almost under siege was extremely demanding. These risks, these vicissitudes, these fortunes of war were faced equally by Royal Navy escort vessels and merchantmen alike. There was not one death for one category and another for another. At least death was impartial.

London to Methil to Clyde, Tail-o'-the Bank

The run around the top of Great Britain from the Clyde to Loch Ewe and Methil, coded 'WN', presaging his later route to North Russia, was a home-run convoy Brundle did several times. It was all part of the overriding purpose of transporting coal to where it was needed, so that when the ships in convoy bunkered they were doing this with a measure of safety and security. Southend to Methil, coded 'FS', was another popular run. It must have seemed as if every vessel near to or in reach of a British port was perpetually on the move, most of them in small convoys, for destroyers and Royal Navy escorts needed more and more coal. Warships big and small bunkered at Tail-o'-the-Bank, the Clyde anchorage, so merchant vessels of all kinds beat a steady path up the Firth of Clyde to Tail-o'-the-Bank. These anchorages, as long as they had a steady and regular amount of coal supplied, were indeed, in a manner of speaking, the arteries of the nation. The convoys never ceased. Night and day, near and far, they were always on the go. They plied their trade. They were a perpetual motion machine. The convoys were always out, and did not rest by day or night.

The reputation of the Russian run, the Murmansk run, was fearsome, and every allied seaman must have known that sooner or later he would have to make a trip to North Russia. For naval escorts with the Home Fleet at Scapa Flow, for merchant seamen, signing on in the 'Pool', Russia loomed. It filled horizons in those days. It paralleled the Atlantic battle, this battle of the Arctic from mid-1941 onwards.

Some historians, looking at the two battles and putting this part of the conflict in perspective, treat the run to Russia as a part of the battle of the Atlantic. The North Cape and its potential for convoys being attacked in its vicinity was ineluctably linked with the pattern and movement of convoys in the North Atlantic. The arrival of vessels across the Atlantic with goods and material earmarked for Russia, and waiting there in Iceland for their convoy to appear, coming up from Loch Ewe, were part of the same sphere of operations as the Arctic operations and as those actions that were unfolding in and around the Kola inlet. The timing of convoys going out west or east, or coming back east or west had to accommodate the same criteria of serviceability and availability. And yet convoy battles and convoy needs were reluctant to be confined, or even defined by reference to an Atlantic-Arctic axis. At one point in the story of the Russian convoys the overriding needs of the Malta convoys were such that escort vessels had to part company with their escorted convoy ships, as soon as various key danger zones had been surmounted and sailed through. There were three needy points of supply, the UK, the North Russian ports and Malta itself, and every one of these three areas depended upon the Home Fleet, sometimes (indeed, increasingly often) augmented by help, when all three areas were needing succour at the same time, from the escort vessels of the Western Approaches. To those involved with the problems of logistics and supply you could not separate the Atlantic, the Arctic and Malta as separate battles, although it was manifestly easier to consider Atlantic and Arctic convoys together.

Over the top of the world

Churchill promised Stalin a convoy every ten days 'counting on Archangel to handle the bulk of the deliveries'. This took no account of the fact that Archangel, further south on the White Sea, and 400 miles further on than Murmansk, was iced up throughout the winter months. Murmansk had an ice-free anchorage due to the warmth of the North Atlantic Drift ocean current. Murmansk was therefore the port of first resort for the convoys, even though its facilities left a lot to be desired, and the port had difficulties in handling the increased traffic the convoys brought.

In the winter months there was darkness along the route of the Russian run for the whole twenty-four hours. The weather in the winter months was truly appalling, 60 degrees of frost but without freezing, and a wind that comes screaming off the Greenland icecap. Spray crashed on the deck as solid ice. Flesh that touched frozen metal stuck to it and peeled off, causing a nasty injury. And the men, for all the Arctic waistcoats and clothing, found it hard to keep warm.

In the summer months, there was no cloak of darkness to protect the ships of the convoy. Instead it was daylight for twenty-four hours, a 'white night', often of unbroken sunshine, with all the vulnerability for a convoy that that would entail. But summer had its compensations. The limit of ice in summer months meant that they could take a more northerly route, and so distance themselves from the German-held airfields in Norway, as well as from surface shipping in the Norwegian fiords. And as their destination the convoy would use one of the White Sea ports, Archangel or Molotovsk.

One of the most perilous journeys of the war

The Russian run, the journey of the Russian convoys to Murmansk or Archangel, was one of the most perilous journeys of the war. The weather was the supreme enemy, with ships growing top-heavy because of the ice building up on them, and hence becoming vulnerable to capsizing. Ships' weapons systems froze up, and the men needed to remain alert to attacks from German aircraft from the Norwegian coast, U-boats, or even surface shipping from the Norwegian fiords. It was fearfully difficult for a heavily laden merchant vessel to keep station in mountainous Arctic seas.

Iceland – a necessary haven

Iceland was crucial as a staging port, and as a refuelling facility. From May 1940 it had been occupied by British and Canadian troops, but in 1941, when the convoys began, was largely garrisoned by the Americans. Outside the capital, Reykjavik, was the large anchorage of Hvalfiordur, where the ships of the convoy would gather and wait for their escorts. Here also American ships that had made an Atlantic crossing but were destined for North Russia would wait for their convoy to come in from their UK port of call.

There was always among the Icelanders a residual ill feeling towards the allies. We had invaded them, and the Americans had made the occupancy enduring, semi-permanent even. For most of 1940 the Icelanders did not speak to British service-men. Troops drooled over the blonde Icelandic ice maidens; but there was mostly nothing doing in that direction. Relationships thawed, as relationships always do, when the Americans arrived, for Uncle Sam wouldn't take 'no' for an answer.

There wasn't much to do with a 48-hour pass in Reykjavik. It was like a shanty town from the wild west, with lots of build-ings of corrugated iron. There were cultural pursuits, chamber concerts at the cathedral, a bookshop with some English titles. Auden and Isherwood, in their celebrated visit to Iceland, had patronised it. Sherry was consumed in liberal quantities. It seemed to be the only drink around. Not much here, then, for the lower deck.

In 1941 the Americans changed all this. Saturday-night dances at the Hotel Borg, a flood of goods from the PX that were otherwise prohibitive while the war was on brought a general thawing-out of relationships all round.

And then there was the austere Icelandic landscape to go for walks in, a setting for many of those Old Norse sagas. Ships, escort ships, merchant ships used Iceland for her deep fiords, which would accommodate fairly large numbers of ships. So the Germans had Norway, we had Iceland.

Hvalfiordur, however, was certainly no adequate shelter from wind and storm. It was, rather, a highly exposed anchorage. Its usefulness as an assembly point for convoys lay in its proximity to Reykjavik. Seidisfiord, in the east of the island, was another Icelandic anchorage used by the allies, particularly by Royal Navy escorts waiting for their convoys. Like Hvalfiordur, Seidisfiord promised 'nought for your comfort'.

The Icelandic anchorages on the way to North Russia had a provisional and temporary quality to them. The demands of war and of the Russian run had brought all these ships to this island, nothing else.

A convoy every ten days

In the early days of the convoys the Royal Navy, together with the MOWT, maintained and sent off a convoy to Russia every ten days. And so a return convoy, QP-3, would sail homewards from Archangel on 27 November, and, ten days after PQ-4 had left Hvalfiordur in Iceland, another convoy, PQ-5, would leave Hvalfiordur also, only just breaking into the Gourlo Strait into the White Sea and Archangel with the help of Russian icebreakers. Convoy PQ-6, the next convoy, was too late to arrive at Archangel. The strait was blocked. It had to make do with Murmansk.

The urgency behind the British promises of a regular 'shuttle' of these convoys is reflected in the contemporary dilemma the Russians were in, with the Nazis at the gates of Moscow on 2 October and Leningrad under siege. Soon after the first in the PQ- series, convoy PQ-1, had set out for Russia, on 26 September 1941, Churchill stated that the UK's entire tank production for that month would be sent to Russia. The British were straining every muscle to keep Russia fighting Hitler. This impressed itself notably and vividly on those who carried the cargoes to Russia and especially on the men of convoy PQ-6, who had hoped to arrive at Archangel before the ice denied them access.

Robert Brundle was with convoy PQ-6, as Master of the SS *Harmatris*. He completed loading a special cargo at Port Glasgow on 27 November 1941, cast off moorings and sailed down the River Clyde towards Gourock Bay, anchoring there until 3.15pm the next day waiting for a convoy to turn up. It was not until 9.45pm on 3 December that the crew of *Harmatris* hove up and proceeded in convoy to Iceland.

Iceland was reached and the convoy waited in Hvalfiordur near Reykjavik, leaving there on 8 December. The convoy PQ-6 consisted of nine ships, a Panamanian tanker, *El Oceano*, and another Panamanian ship, *Mount Evans*, with five British merchant vessels, *Harmatris, Explorer, Empire Mavis, El Mirlo* and *Elona* (the Commodore ship), the rescue ship, *Zamalek*, and a Russian vessel, *Dekabrist*.

Robert Brundle: Previous convoys

The war had impinged in hectic fashion on the life of Robert Brundle and on those who sailed with him in *Harmatris* as it had on the lives of all merchant seamen. Before this Murmansk adventure, Brundle had sailed in September in OS-5, a convoy from Liverpool to Freetown, Sierra Leone and back. Earlier in the year he had sailed in one of the Atlantic convoys to North America, and back in HX-139, from Halifax, Nova Scotia to Liverpool. The previous year, 1940, he had sailed with a cargo of ballast to fetch a cargo from the River Plate, and not long before made another trip from Liverpool to Durban, South Africa. He and the crew of *Harmatris* were getting used to seeing the Liver building dominating their home port. In fact this poor old home port was getting knocked about. In 1940 and 1941 bombings of British cities by the Luftwaffe were at their height, and after the London blitz provincial cities like Liverpool, Hull, Birmingham, Southampton and Glasgow were visited nightly by German bombers. Hull, Glasgow and Liverpool, in particular, because they were premium ports, were very badly bombed. I have met folk from Hull whose entire family were wiped out in the bombing. Often on returning to Liverpool, Brundle and the convoy would be diverted or instructed to heave to, and wait, because an air raid was in progress.

From 'my Liverpool home' to a base on the Clyde

The key port for the departure of Atlantic convoys during this period was, of course, Liverpool, the HQ of what was known as the Western Approaches. Up to 1943 the Germans were sinking British and allied ships at a rate faster than they could be replaced. Happily the tide turned for both the Atlantic and Arctic convoys in 1943. Liberty ships, built by Henry Kaiser, were flooding off the assembly lines in the USA, Canada and Britain, the escort vessels of the Royal Navy were developing a proficient and effective defence strategy (and there were more of these escorts being built and commissioned), and, although the convoys suffered casualties to the very end, they were winning through with fewer of their ships lost.

After service with Atlantic convoys, in North or South Atlantic, the Russian convoys started, and, at a stroke Brundle's home port was moved from the Mersey and Liverpool to the Clyde and Port Glasgow. The organisation and maintenance of the Russian convoys was in the hands of the Home Fleet at Scapa Flow, although the ships departing for North Russia generally assembled, as we shall see, at Loch Ewe, in the north-west of Scotland, before sailing for Iceland.

Brundle and *Harmatris* turn back from PQ-6; the convoy goes on to Murmansk and Archangel

Two ships of PQ-6 were forced to turn back, one, my grand-father's ship, the SS *Harmatris*, because of a fire on board and the SS *Zamalek*, a rescue ship, which turned back to assist *Harmatris*.

The convoy, when they were gathered together in Iceland, must have speculated, as they waited, over their chances of reaching Archangel before the ice imprisoned them. For, as we have seen, the convoy was to be too late to arrive in Archangel. A fierce south-westerly gale blew up, and a storm began to rage, a storm which placed obstacles in the way of PQ-6's smooth and timely arrival at her destination, and during which two ships were detached from the convoy.

Brundle and *Harmatris*, one of the two ships in question, fell behind the convoy, and hove to, prepared to ride the storm out. The fire that was discovered on their ship, and which they fought long and hard to save the ship's cargo and the crew's lives, forms the subject of the next chapter. Meanwhile, the storm was the main enemy, something to fight with every ounce of courage and endeavour.

Arctic storm

Mere words do not do justice to the violence of the Arctic storm that frustrated the arrival of PQ-6 into Archangel before the ice made the passage impossible. The wind was over 120 knots, and the noise, a shrieking and a roaring, was terrific. Ships could do nothing but battle the weather, and stay afloat. This was a time for injuries as men were flung on deck. The very rivets of the ship, basic Clyde rivets, vibrated, left their places and were lost. *Harmatris* yawed over, far over on the starboard side; other ships listed to port. Forecastles disappeared in a wall of water that enveloped the entire ship.

Throughout the duration of a storm like this one the men were hungry, as well as seasick, for after prolonged seasickness the appetite recovers. But how could anyone eat a meal when a ship rolled to an angle of 30 degrees, or even 50 degrees? Stewards below deck fought to keep crockery and eating utensils battened beneath the hatches, since, after the overwhelming, the prime urge to preserve life and limb, it is the little things, the food and associated comforts that count for much. But when anemometers were registering gusts of over 125mph, men could do nothing except shut down, batten down and steer into the eye of the storm, and avoid injury. For Arctic weather could render a cut or sore, incurred by being blown onto one of the many sharp corners or objects with which any ship was liberally provided, infected in a relatively short time, both by the extreme cold and exposure to freezing surfaces.

Snow blown onto the decks and superstructures of ships rapidly became ice, to the tune of at first several tons, and eventually hundreds of tons. A vessel with a high centre of gravity rolls in a way that is totally unstable, and several ships in several convoys in a number of vicious storms like this one rolled back and back, past the point of return, and were engulfed by the restless ocean and the horrendous waves. Thankfully this did not occur to any of the handful of stalwart ships in PQ-6, though the men on board expected it, with every roll.

The evidence that they had been in a kind of Arctic hell was clear to see, when the winds died and the waves returned to a more normal level. Apart from a variety of damage to masts, funnels and superstructures, something which kept carpenters and little knots of crew members busy for a good while, there were those tell-tale signs, under the dull white Arctic camouflage paint, of streaks, of great swathes of red lead, as if, out of all the banshees shrieking round these ships, one or two of them had taken preternaturally large scraping implements and scraped the long sides of several ships down to the dull, rusty leaden surface, which contrasted so vividly and even shockingly with the bland, white 'hostilities-only' wartime paint, which many ships, though not all, were clad in.

Some men, only a very few, had encountered an Arctic storm before. They were not surprised by its ferocity, although the one that struck and almost overwhelmed PQ-6 was one of the worst they had encountered. They were the men who had sailed the trawlers from Hull, Grimsby, Fleetwood and the Scottish ports. Some of them were found in crews of merchantmen, though sometimes entire trawler crews and trawlers converted to military purposes went to the war. Often peacetime trawler experience proved invaluable to some in the current Arctic emergency.

Trawlers and 'pleasuring' and tips for the real war

It was, for example, a real Arctic emergency that brought out a piece of solid trawler experience on the part of a former peacetime barrister who had metamorphosed into the wartime figure (like putting on a mask, almost) of Lieutenant Leo Joseph Anthony Gradwell RNVR. The occasion for Gradwell to use this item of arcane trawler knowledge came about in the dire set of circumstances of July 1942, during convoy PQ-17, when the Admiralty signal 'Convoy is to scatter' was received, and merchant vessels plunged like lemmings in all directions, and U-boats picked them off, in an almost indecent leisurely fashion.

Robert Brundle heard about this utter calamity, while he was waiting at Archangel for a convoy home, surrounded as he was, on all sides, by refugees from PQ-17, some of whom he was to provide passage home for on the eventful convoy, QP-14.

Gradwell used to spend some of his peacetime holidays away from his busy life as a barrister as a passenger on some of the trawlers that sailed from Hull and Grimsby into those waters around Bear Island – 'Pleasuring', it was called, as if to say that people take their pleasure in different ways, there being no accounting for taste. He vastly enjoyed the icy seas, and talked with well-travelled, hard-bitten trawlermen. All this, after all, is what brought him, when the call to arms came, into the RNVR. He knew, from these talks, just how near the pack ice around Bear Island they could go without damage to his ship, an Asdic trawler, HMS *Ayrshire*. He had been to Bear Island a few times on his pleasuring trips. The ice protected German detection methods from penetrating around Bear Island. He took with him, when the convoy scattered, three merchant ships, and he and they lined up against the ice. He had some white and pale-green paint aboard and instructed the men to paint their sides with this superb piece of camouflage. As there was not enough paint to go round, crews finished up painting one side of their ship only, as paint was strictly rationed. They were invisible to the Blohm und Voss spotter aircraft, and they survived the carnage erupting all round them. Lieutenant Gradwell nursed his little convoy into the security of the White Sea.

The Gourlo Strait or Murmansk

Fighting the storm with every ounce of their strength and capability, and despite the well-advised turning back of *Harmatris* with the rescue ship *Zamalek*, convoy PQ-6 had found the entrance to the White Sea, the painfully narrow Gourlo Strait, with the rest of the convoy, her escorts, HMS *Edinburgh* and two destroyers, *Echo* and *Escapade*. It was decided to detach *El Mirlo* and the Russian *Dekabrist* to go back to Murmansk, while the minesweepers HMS *Speedy* and *Hazard* saw the rest of the convoy into the White Sea port of Molotovsk. There was a third mine-sweeper, HMS *Leda*, involved also, as HMS *Speedy* had been hit (without sustaining casualties, fortunately) by German destroyers, themselves laying mines on the approaches to Molotovsk. PQ-6 was characterised by a number of hostile encounters with the Germans, who were waking up to the strategic implications of the convoys.

Russian icebreakers were active in assisting the major part of PQ-6, five ships, all except for *El Mirlo* and *Dekabrist*, to reach Molotovsk. This small White Sea port was reached on 28 December, only for the five ships, together with their Russian icebreaker, to remain ice-locked until the following June. Murmansk was crammed full of allied vessels, and it was politic to take away from the bombing those ships that could be accommodated in other ports.

The Russian ship *Dekabrist,* one of only two ships from PQ-6 to have diverted to Murmansk, sailed straightaway into a Murmansk bombing raid. Shepherded into Murmansk by HMS *Echo,* one of her destroyer escorts, she was attacked by two Junkers 88s and left with two unexploded bombs on her decks. The cruiser HMS *Edinburgh* and six Russian Hurricanes drove away the Ju 88s. Finally the bombs on the deck of *Dekabrist* were dealt with, and *Edinburgh* and *Echo,* picking up their pilots on 20 December, anchored 4 miles below Murmansk.

PQ-6 suffered numerous acts of harassment and attacks on the approaches to Murmansk. That was why the bulk of the convoy was accommodated in Molotovsk, because of Murmansk's extreme vulnerability to air attack, and, as we shall see later in this book, the paucity of proper equipment to lift the heavy cargoes, not to mention the lack of space for vessels to berth.

PQ-6 was nevertheless still a lucky convoy. PQ-8, which we shall hear about as part of the story of *Harmatris,* was the first Russian convoy to take heavy casualties, the loss of a destroyer with all her ship's company except for two, and in a number of ways was to presage the subsequent strain and casualty-fraught lives of those who embarked on the Russian run.

PQ-7A

PQ-6 was the first discrete convoy to which the Germans offered offensive action. After the safe arrival of PQ-6 in North Russia, it was the turn of what the naval planners called PQ-7A, two ships, detached from what would have been a much larger convoy. One ship, the SS *Waziristan,* left Iceland on 26 December 1941 and became separated, both from her escorts and from her other companion ship, *Cold Harbour,* flying the flag of Panama. She was stranded on the edge of the polar ice field, where she was torpedoed by *U-134* on 2 January 1942, and sank. Forty-seven men, including ten DEMS (Defensively Equipped Merchant Ships) gunners perished.

As for those who arrived in a convoy at Murmansk, after the variety of experiences they had endured on the convoy, like the crews of the PQ-6 ships, they became used to small mercies. The main thing was that they were there, in port, alive and with their cargoes intact. They were going to have to cope and survive on a very little during their enforced stay in one of these benighted North Russian ports. The same situation awaited Robert Brundle and the crew of *Harmatris* on a future convoy, PQ-8.

CHAPTER 4

Fire Amidships

Sea Shanty

Chorus:
Fire Down Below
Fire, fire, fire down below
So fetch a bucket of water, lads,
It's fire down below.

There is a fire in the lower hold,
There's a fire down below,
Fire in the main well,
The captain didn't know.

Chorus

There is fire in the forepeak,
Fire in the main,
Fire in the windlass,
Fire in the chain.

Chorus

There is fire in the foretop,
Fire down below,
Fire in the chain-plates,
The bosun didn't know.

Chorus

49

There is fire up aloft,
There is fire down below
Fire in the galley,
The cook he didn't know.

Chorus

Fighting the Fire

PQ-6 had left Hvalfiordur on 8 December only to be overtaken by the aforementioned fierce storm which raged for two days. In this storm and in this convoy, however, *Harmatris* was to experience a problem all her own. At about 11.20pm, the captain was told that the deck adjacent to No. 2 hold was hot, and that steam was coming up out of it. The water lying on the deck above No. 4 'tweendeck was issuing as vapour, and rapidly becoming steam.

Crew members cautiously lifted up the corner of the hatch, and they could make out in the gloom and among the steam a lorry, full of NAAFI stores, loose from its bindings and fastenings, careering on fire across the 'tweendeck. The ship itself was being shaken in the maw of the storm, and was rolling almost uncontrollably. The motion of the ship caused the lorry to slam into other stowed items of cargo with the result that bales and cases were broken open, so that the burning lorry set alight even more of the ship's cargo.

Robert Brundle went aft immediately to the site of the incident leaving the Third Officer Mr Watson in charge of the bridge. There he gave orders to Mr G.E. Masterman, the Chief Officer, to drench the hold with steam, to take off the port ventilator and to use the chemical extinguishers. At the forward end the hatch was opened, and a rope ladder lowered down. The Chief Officer, Masterman, was a 41-year-old West Hartlepool man, and he went down the temporary ladder dragging a hose, seeking to direct water on the lorry. He toiled at this dangerous job for some time before, even though he was wearing a mask, the fumes overcame him.

Fortunately there was a safety line tied round his body, as part of normal safety procedure, and willing hands hauled him out of the smoke-filled hatch before he lost consciousness and collapsed. The smoke helmet was, at best, a primitive form of breathing apparatus, which a bellows and hose kept supplied with air from the outside.

It must be emphasised that there were normally two possibilities for dealing with a shipboard fire, the first to take to the boats and escape the fire, the second to fight it. This second choice was the only one to adopt in this wartime emergency, first because the mountainous waves of the storm made taking to the lifeboats practically impossible and extremely hazardous, and secondly because they must save the fire from getting to the ten tons of cordite and large quantities of small arms and ammunition stowed between the 'tweendecks in the hold. The fire must be mastered, and there was no other choice. To let the fire reach the cordite was to risk losing the ship, and the lives of a good proportion of the crew.

After the Chief Officer had been relieved, Chief Steward R. Peart, a younger man in his early twenties from South Wales, had a spell with the fire helmet and the hose until he too was overcome by fumes. But still the fire continued, and the lorry and the adjacent cargo blazed away.

Brundle had to think of the lives of his crew, and not just of the cargo. The storm showed no signs of abating, but they now needed a ship standing by for assistance. He therefore instructed the Radio Officer, Mr J. Delaney, to send a message to the Senior Escort Officer asking for help, no matter that this broke the rule of radio silence.

Zamalek and Harmatris

Sailing with PQ-6 at this time was the rescue ship SS *Zamalek*, whose captain announced that she was proceeding to the assistance of *Harmatris* at 2 knots per hour, her maximum speed. *Zamalek*, built in the 1920s, was a former Egyptian mail-line ship of only 1,567 tons. She and *Zaafaran* played a significant part in providing rescue services (she was fitted up with medical facilities and had medical personnel sailing with her) for stricken ships in a number of critical convoys. Contrast the Mediterranean short-shuttle work these ships did in their former existence with their new, enhanced role of the Russian convoys in the Arctic seas.

Both *Zaafaran* and *Zamalek* were originally captured from a German company, the Pharaonic Mail Line, and had been managed by the General Steam Navigation Company, while they plied their trade as Thames Pleasure Cruises. So it was from the Nile to the Thames to the Arctic for *Zamalek* and *Zaafaran*.

Meanwhile, Brundle and Peart took turns to fight the fire for the rest of the night in the 'tweendecks, dodging the lorries careering about, and braving the fire and smoke, seeking to quench the blaze before it reached the cordite and the ammunition. The heaving, high seas made their task doubly difficult.

By the early hours of the morning of 9 December the danger was almost over. The fire seemed under control, although there was much damping down to do. By the evening at 7.30pm it was finally extinguished.

Robert Brundle thanked *Zamalek*, which had been standing by, awaiting, it can be imagined, a probable fearful outcome on *Harmatris*, and asked the ship to rejoin the convoy. Brundle also sent a message to the convoy Senior Escort Officer, asking permission to return to Glasgow, and there to have a thorough examination of the fire damage and a restowing of the cargo. Permission was readily granted for this, and so the ship was turned round, still in the teeth of the gales blowing up from the storm. Always the storm.

Back to the Clyde

In order to return to port in those fierce weather conditions, some attempt had to be made to secure the cargo in No. 2 hold. This was done, and the cargo in the other holds was made safe. And so it was back through the Minches, and *Harmatris* arrived at Rothesay Anchorage far down the Firth of Clyde at 3.30pm on 9 December.

At the anchorage officers from the Naval Control of Shipping Organisation (NCSO) were waiting to board. The Naval Control of Shipping officers handled movement of ships in the ports where convoys assembled; they checked for faulty stores etc., and in every way acted as intermediaries between the Master of the vessel, her owners, and the Admiralty.

On the next day, 10 December, Robert Brundle made his report to Captain May RN and other NCSO officials. He had to give the reasons for his early return, and also to inform the owner, J. & C. Harrison of London. His actions and decisions were upheld and vindicated, and *Harmatris* was sent, with the blessing of the owners and the Admiralty, back to Queen's Dock, Glasgow.

Cargo discharge and Christmas Day

Here began the discharge of the cargo, a process in which the Master was intimately and thoroughly involved. It was, as can be imagined, not a normal discharge of cargo. That took long enough as it was, but this damaged and battered cargo needed to be discharged, examined, restowed, relashed, and made secure, with several items needing to be replaced and renewed. All this took the captain and crew until Christmas.

After an inspection by the captain, on Boxing Day morning, 26 December, the SS *Harmatris*, shaking off the experiences of false starts and fire, set sail. There was a feeling of hope, and thanksgiving for deliverance from the fire, which had so nearly accounted for the lives of the crew and the ship. There had been a good celebration of Christmas the day before with the steward and stewarding staff excelling themselves to produce a good Christmas dinner for the crew, who were confined to the ship. There was to be no home leave or visiting of families. Most of them had last seen families a month ago, before the sailing of PQ-6 on 27 November. They were not to see families again for nearly nine months, did they but know it.

Harmatris casts off moorings from the riverside quay at Port Glasgow, and sails down the Clyde to Gourock Bay

From Greenock to Gourock Bay the freighter moved, picking up, as an escort, the minesweeper HMS *Northern Spray* at Tail-o'-the-Bank, the anchorage for destroyers, minesweepers and other RN vessels between Greenock and Gourock.

Greenock was a pretty town with views across the Gareloch. It was famous as the birthplace of the pirate-hunter turned pirate, Captain William Kidd, who was executed in 1701. More relevant to Brundle and other merchant ships was that Greenock's other famous son was James Watt, eighteenth-century inventor of the steam engine. Most merchant ships in the convoys were powered by steam. War had brought Greenock to prominence and, for the most part, for all its prettiness, it was as unprepossessing as the ships that passed through it, except for a touch of wartime glamour the previous month, tragic in retrospect, when HMS *Prince of Wales* and HMS *Repulse* passed through on their way (did their crews but know it) to a shocking watery doom in the seas off the coast of Malaya (now Malaysia).

Degaussing and adjusting compasses

At Gourock some work had to be done before *Harmatris* could be committed to the seas. First the compasses were adjusted. The ship's compasses were corrected for deviation, caused by the excess magnetism that had built up in the instrument since the last correction or adjustment. To do this the ship was taken round successive compass points, objects on shore with a known magnetic bearing, and the reading of the compass corrected accordingly. Next the vessel went over the DG (degaussing) range to be wiped clean of any future perilous attentions from German limpet or magnetic mines.

The degaussing process was so-called because, ironically, a German scientist of the past called Gauss had discovered and demonstrated the process in physics that lay at the heart of this modern twentieth-century operation. Before setting out on a convoy a ship approached the DG range, which in the case of *Harmatris* was in Gourock Bay, and a cable was passed around the ship by other ships present. This reduced or, at least, neutralised German magnetic mines and limpet mines. It proved highly effective, and became a regular prelude to fitting out a ship for convoy work or for any major and lengthy operation that took her into dangerous enemy waters.

From Clyde to Loch Ewe

The Firth of Clyde becomes easier on the eye the more a ship ventures towards its mouth: the hills of Hunter's Quay and Rothesay, the islands of Little Cumbrae and Great Cumbrae, Gourock Head and southwards for Holy Island. After Ailsa Craig *Harmatris* swung round the Mull of Kintyre and out to the Minches, those channels between the Hebridean islands, beautiful even with the weather running to strong winds and rough seas, as it was on this journey.

Between the isles of Skye and North and South Uist there was a passage for *Harmatris* of 21km. Known as The Little Minch, this gives the ships access to the next passage, known as The Great Minch or North Minch, threading her way again between islands, between Lewis and Harris and the mainland. This was, indeed, a maritime 'Road to the Isles'.

And so, escorted by HMS *Northern Spray*, *Harmatris* came to Loch Ewe. This was by now the classic and standard point of assembly to Russia. Far beyond it to the north-east, around Cape Wrath and through the waters of the Pentland Firth lay the magnificent anchorage of Scapa Flow. Scapa Flow had been the home of Admiral Jellicoe's Grand Fleet, which had left this peaceful anchorage one evening in May of 1916 to meet the German High Seas Fleet in what became known as the Battle of Jutland. From Scapa also, on another night in 1916, Field Marshall Lord Kitchener left on the cruiser *Hampshire* to go to Archangel for crucial talks with the Russians, only to meet his end in those waters after his ship struck a mine. Meanwhile, twenty-six years after these climactic events, there were other ships getting ready to sail from Scapa Flow to Arctic waters. HMS *Matabele* and HMS *Somali* were being fitted out and were preparing to sail from Scapa to Iceland, then to refuel at Seidisfiord before meeting their convoy, PQ-8, when they sailed from Hvalfiordur. Scapa Flow was, at the time of the convoys to Russia, the headquarters of the Home Fleet. The Home Fleet supplied escorts for the Russian convoys. They looked eastwards, as the Western Approaches ships of Liverpool looked westwards. They had to keep eyes open, as well, for *Tirpitz* and other German capital ships in the Norwegian fiords. Their counterpart, the Western Approaches fleet, did the same for the Atlantic convoys and for enemy activity in this area to the west. Usually Royal Navy escort vessels held a rendezvous with their convoy at one of the Icelandic harbours or anchorages.

Harmatris was making for Loch Ewe, there to join and make up, with other vessels, the convoy PQ-8.

Loch Ewe – last port for Russia

Loch Ewe, in Wester Ross on the Atlantic Coast of Scotland, is 10 miles long by 4 miles wide. Safe anchorage could be provided for up to forty ships at any one time, which made it an ideal assembly point for ships setting off for North Russia.

It contains some of the most arresting mountain scenery in the whole of the country, easy to defend and so festooned with coastal defence batteries, constantly manned when the convoys were in the loch. A tiny pub, The Aultbea Inn, was the only place of entertainment. The landlord ran out of glasses when the ships were gathering and served his beer from jam jars. For this reason this last and remote hostelry on the mainland of Britain was known by the convoy crews, and is known to this day, as 'The Jam Jar Inn'.

On the shores of the loch at Rubha Nan Sason there is a worthy memorial to the convoy men who sailed from here, erected by the Veterans' body, the Russian Convoy Club, in September 1999.

The wording is a poignant reminder of a last look at all things lovely (to echo the poem of Walter de la Mare) by crews of merchant ships and Royal Navy escorts who sailed from this beautiful loch into fiery trials in the Arctic Ocean:

> *In memory of our shipmates, who sailed from Loch Ewe during World War II. They lost their lives in the bitter Arctic sea battles to North Russia and never returned to this tranquil anchorage. We will always remember them.*

Brundle had to attend a conference in Loch Ewe, with the other captains and radio officers of all the merchant vessels making up the convoy. There was a hut alongside the Jam Jar

Inn, with plenty of space and seating accommodation, where the conference took place. Otherwise it doubled as the Officers' Mess. The man conducting the briefing was the convoy escort commander, referred to in signals as Comescort, or his representative. Maps were pulled down in front of a blackboard, and the route to North Russia was pointed out, on a map of the Norwegian and Barents seas from Greenland to Novaya Zemlya. To the North there was a shaded area indicating the limits of the pack ice. This forced the convoy, in the months of the winter season, to sail further south than ships and crews wished, as it put them nearer to the hostile Norwegian coast, from which enemy aircraft could take off and harass the convoy.

Convoy conference

The conference room was fairly crowded with chairs along the walls of the hut, and long benches in the body of the hut. Some of the Masters wore their uniform; others attended in dark suits, with overcoats or trilby hats or homburgs; 'owners rig', as they called this among their fraternity, that is what they would wear to visit their ship's owners in port, an abiding testimony to their civilian identity, whatever the war would throw in their direction.

Godfrey and Roger, the celebrated brothers Winn

Godfrey Winn, the journalist, who, for part of the war, became an ordinary seaman and who wrote a searching and sensitive book on PQ-17, spoke of attending a convoy conference at Western Approaches Command at Liverpool. He commented on the civilian suits the merchant captains and first officers wore for the conference. 'There was not a uniform among them' was Winn's comment, while, evidently, someone, one of their number, was actually wearing galoshes, 'as though he of all people should be worried about getting his feet wet on shore'. Certainly these civilians afloat worked hard for their crews, worked hard for their company, and as their grievous losses show, deserved well of their country.

Before Godfrey Winn joined up as an ordinary seaman, he was a civilian newspaper reporter and columnist. He had an opportunity to accompany a Russian convoy after joining the converted merchant steamer turned AA cruiser HMS *Pozarica*. So Winn was in fact the only newspaperman allowed to travel on the North Russian run.

His book on PQ-17, which was the convoy destiny bestowed on him to report on for his newspaper, is one of the best of a number of books written about this tragic convoy. What he never mentions is the role of his brother, Commander Roger Winn. In civilian life he was a barrister, Roger Winn QC, a talented barrister with a back twisted from an early brush with polio, which frustrated an ambition to join the Royal Navy. In the war-time RNVR Roger Winn ran the STR at Naval HQ, the Submarine Tracking Room of the Admiralty Operational Intelligence Centre. He seemed to possess, all those who worked with him attest, some kind of sixth sense, an uncanny ability to judge and guess what Dönitz's intentions were, and how the submarines were going to behave.

It is astonishing to recall how much these two brothers, the naval commander and the ordinary seaman, in their very different ways, contributed to the naval war effort. Godfrey Winn had a soft spot for the Merchant Navy, for the men of the Red Duster. He often lamented that neither had their story been sufficiently or imaginatively told, nor their co-operation with the senior service in the long war put into any kind of perspective. It is to be hoped that this narrative will go some way towards fulfilling this postponed objective.

The conference itself took a fair time. The route, order of steaming, speed of the convoy, and any special instructions about signals were covered, with time after each section of the briefing for questions and observations.

The convoy route

The convoy route was time-honoured. Changes reflected the seasons of the year. They were to sail from Loch Ewe to Iceland. Thence (and this would no doubt be the subject of another conference at Hvalfiordur) up Iceland's west coast, and they would turn north-east. There they would be joined by the full complement of the escorts. From Jan Mayen Island to Bear Island, on the longitude of the North Cape (51 degrees E) the close escorts would protect them, minesweepers from the 6th Minesweeping Flotilla, based at the Kola inlet, up to Murmansk.

The projected intelligence about U-boats and their expected location, as well as minefields sown by our own side was given. The number and composition of the escort ships of the Royal Navy were touched upon, and the necessity for radio silence, unless attacked, was underlined.

There were words about those who could not make the requisite number of knots, who hung back and were therefore a burden on the escort vessels, which, instead of sailing to port or starboard, on either beam of the merchant vessels, had to go out and help them, even if this meant hanging back. There was a drill for rescuing a ship, even though there was a kind of cerebral hopelessness about it.

Every effort was made to drive home the conviction that the convoy would be protected, and to underline how each escort vessel would play their part in this. The fact that PQ-8, in common with other convoys at this time, was small by comparison added a special edge to the warnings and reassurances and outright blandishments. They were a little family almost, and everyone's welfare was in the hands of everyone else. They, the Masters and crewmen, sought to bring these cargoes in. They were tired, but they were intensely focussed. Newcomers to Arctic routes and convoys took endless notes. As for the old hands, they had passed this way before.

Close of conference for PQ-8

At the end of the conference the necessity of keeping to the prescribed speed was highlighted, as well as the dangers of straggling and, hence, of creating smoke. Comescort, the convoy escort commander, wished everyone the best, and the ships' Masters and radio officers dispersed.

There had been a measure of good-humoured banter at the outset of the conference and before it started. Leaving the conference, the men seemed subdued, apprehensive, perhaps, over what lay ahead, and aware of the nature and extent of their responsibilities. A few waited around, mutually checking and rechecking details they had been given. Their experience and professionalism would be tested to the utmost in the days ahead.

CHAPTER 5

Three Torpedoes and Two Air Attacks

There go the ships, and there is that Leviathan, whom thou hast made to take his pastime therein

Psalm 104:26

Thrice I suffered shipwreck, a night and a day I have been in the deep; in journeyings often, in perils of waters ... in perils in the sea ... in weariness and painfulness, in watchings often, in hunger and thirst, in fastings often

2 Corinthians 11: 25–27

Ships and men in PQ-8

There were two British tankers in convoy PQ-8, *British Pride* and *British Workman*, and then the steamers *Dartford* and *Southgate*. There were also *El Amirante*, flying the Panamanian flag, but owned and managed by the Americans, and, now that the USA had entered the war, after the Japanese attack on Pearl Harbor earlier that month, the American ship, *Larranga*, which was, in addition, the ship of the Vice Commodore. There was also *Starii Bolshevik* a Russian freighter, and finally *Harmatris*, of which the Master, R.W. Brundle, was appointed Commodore of the convoy for the journey from Loch Ewe to Iceland.

The selection and nationality of ships in this small convoy spoke volumes about the planning and distribution of ships to meet the challenge of the Arctic convoys in their early stages. Here was a small convoy of eight ships. Every ship must count. Every cargo must, if at all possible, get through. Fuel, by this time, was of the utmost importance to the fighting Russians; fuel, and tanks and military vehicles. Hence the presence in the small convoy of eight ships of two British tankers, *British Pride* and *British Workman*, full of fuel, was significant. It was, it goes without saying, an exceptionally dangerous job sailing as the crew of a tanker. When a torpedo struck, it wiped out a part of the crew immediately and irrevocably, without hope of recovery. If there were survivors from a stricken tanker, that was a bonus. Britain did not have a large tanker fleet. Most of them belonged to a tanker line, British Petroleum (BP), which, like these two in PQ-8, had a two-word nomenclature, with the first word being 'British'. So, in addition to *British Pride* and *British Workman* there were *British Patience*, *British Promise*, *British Respect* and *British Valour*, the names exemplifying and embodying the traditional British virtues of grit, perseverance and patriotic excellence contained in the word 'British'. Britain was glad of the influx of more tankers from the free nations, especially the 233 tankers from Norway's merchant fleet when Norway was overrun by the Germans in 1940. They were sorely needed, especially to transport fuel in the Russian run.

The death of a tanker

The death of a tanker torpedoed in a convoy is a spectacular thing, as well as being a horrible thing. Dull, heavy explosions attest to the fact that petrol tanks have gone up. A pervasive crackling plots the course of tons of small-arms ammunition catching fire and going off, just like a firework display.

But there are sights to wake the dead, to fill any sleepless nights with lambent horror for an eternity: a burning sea, a sea on fire from the oil that heaved and shook and reassembled itself because it was alive with men on fire – men on fire, and the sea on fire. When the sea burns, then you have the Apocalypse.

The trouble is that for those hopeless, dying men the agony is inevitably prolonged, for the flames in the burning sea have taken away the oxygen, leaving the men alive enough to suffer death by asphyxiation.

To the men watching all this, to Brundle and the crew in one of the Atlantic convoys of *Harmatris*, it was outrageous, shocking. Men wept, shouted that something must be done for the men in agony; but nothing could be done. Here and there, as they watched the tanker's death agonies, with two parts of the ship pointing to the stars, before sliding down into the watery waste, they could dimly make out individuals in distress, a ship's boy, surrendering his poor tormented body to the deep, a grey-haired old man who should have been on his allotment growing cabbages and dahlias rather than chancing it on board of a massive ship full of crude oil. What a ship, to sail, full astern, in front of the waiting U-boats. It makes you think what people will do for King and Country, what they will do to bring oil, food, ammunition and the rest to keep the war going.

Brundle had seen tankers blown up, several in fact, on the run to Nova Scotia; so had many in the crew of *Harmatris*.

After the two British tankers in this list of eight ships composing PQ-8 there were the three British steamers *Dartford*, *Southgate* and *Harmatris*, all of them between 4,000 and 5,000 tons, and with a good carrying capacity. Like that of *Harmatris*, all their cargoes largely consisted of military vehicles, tanks and even locomotives, and guns, especially anti-aircraft guns, and ammunition.

That left three foreign ships in convoy PQ-8. *El Amirante* was a Panamanian ship flying a flag of convenience, but to all intents and purposes American, as an American shipping company owned and managed her. Panamanian ships were chartered by the MOWT in large numbers earlier in the war, as Britain needed increasing tonnage, and the harvest of ships from the occupied countries, especially from Norway and Greece, had not yet come in.

The presence of the American ship *Larranga*, small by American standards at 3,804 tons, reflects a period before the massive ship-building programme of the USA had got under way. *Larranga*'s membership of PQ-8 was the first time an American ship had sailed openly in an allied convoy without being disguised as Panamanian or by some other special dispensation since America had entered the war a few weeks before. *Starii Bolshevik*, a Russian freighter built in 1937 and weighing 3,974 tons, showed unswerving devotion to duty, both on this convoy and on the other convoys she sailed on, especially on the later convoy PQ-16, when she limped into Murmansk harbour with an impossible amount of bomb damage. Brundle was reminded of her role in PQ-8 when he saw her towed to a berth in Murmansk, and marvelled that she could even stay afloat. So there were two tankers carrying fuel and six freighters with cargoes of military vehicles, guns and ammunition. Boxed aircraft parts were another favourite found in allied cargo holds at this time.

Ships and men in PQ-6

Compare this convoy, in terms of number of ships, type and nationalities with that earlier convoy, PQ-6, in which Brundle began to sail until the fire supervened, and he was forced to return.

PQ-6, like PQ-8, consisted of eight ships. There was one tanker, not two, as in PQ-8, *El Oceano*, flying the Panamanian flag of convenience, as was *Mount Evans*, a freighter, like the other five freighters (which included, remember, *Harmatris* for the initial part of the journey). And so we have *Harmatris, Explorer, Empire Mavis, El Mirlo* and *Elona*, which was the Commodore ship. Last of all, completing the complement of eight ships, was the Russian ship, *Dekabrist*, a very similar tally and makeup (with the absence of any American vessel) to that of PQ-8. Eight escorts were associated (at least in part) with PQ-6, His Majesty's Trawlers *Cape Argona, Hugh Walpole* and *Stella Capella*, two destroyers, HMS *Echo* and *Escapade*, two minesweepers, HMS *Leda* and HMS *Hazard*, and the cruiser HMS *Edinburgh*.

Compare that with the seven ships escorting PQ-8, four Halcyon Class Fleet minesweepers, HMS *Harrier*, HMS *Hazard*, HMS *Sharpshooter* and HMS *Speedwell*; two Tribal Class destroyers, HMS *Matabele* and HMS *Somali*; and HMS *Trinidad*. *Trinidad* was experimental, a new light cruiser with an all-welded hull. Some minds at the Admiralty thought welded constructions unsuitable for the rigour of Arctic weather. PQ-6 and PQ-8 were very similar convoys both in composition and in the firepower of the ships escorting them. Contrast this with the sixty-two Royal Navy ships escorting (at least in part) convoy QP-14, a convoy of twenty vessels. This gives us some idea of the growth and development of the convoy process from December 1941/January 1942, when PQ-6 and PQ-8 sailed, to September 1942, when QP-14 sailed, when an aircraft carrier, HMS *Avenger*, was among the sixty-two escorts.

It is interesting, and an eloquent comment on the American shipbuilding programme and the American drive to create trained seamen, to note that, of the twenty merchant ships of QP-14 nine were American, nine were British, one flew the Panamanian flag and one was Polish. The achievement of PQ-8 was one thing, a testimony to courage, perseverance and determination, in those first tentative steps of the Arctic convoy process, but during the eight months in Murmansk and Archangel Brundle and the crew of *Harmatris* saw, unfolding before their eyes like a *tableau vivant*, the convoy story as it developed, on the move all the time, renewing itself, edging forward, growing. And as the convoys took fearful, even astonishing, casualties, and the constant bombing reinforced this, hammered this home, the Master of *Harmatris* saw the convoy's character changing from that of a smaller convoy of eight ships escorted by an equal number of Royal Navy ships to over twice the number of merchantmen escorted by over seven times the number of Royal Navy ships, with escorts, in a kind of shuttle process, looking after an incoming convoy at fixed points as well as the homeward-bound convoy. It was an amazing enterprise to take part in, assimilate and learn about, more especially against the noisy and dangerous background of Murmansk dock, or that repository of shipwrecked seamen, Archangel, where shoals of the dispossessed, some in real want, thronged the streets and the few places of public resort, grim and febrile though these were.

We have seen at the outset of PQ-8 that Robert Brundle was appointed Commodore of the convoy for the journey from Loch Ewe to Iceland. This was a responsibility he willingly undertook, and also for the next leg of the journey from Iceland to North Russia, though he could have had no idea of the shocks and vicissitudes that would befall him and the crew of *Harmatris*, whose lives he was responsible for, on the journey from Iceland to the entrance to the Kola inlet.

Commodore of PQ-8

At this early stage of the convoy, experienced British merchant captains and shipmasters of proven ability were appointed Commodore, like Brundle. In future convoys retired rear admirals and Captains RN were called out of retirement to do this duty. The Commodore had a role in relation to the other merchant ships in the convoy. He had to see to it that they kept station, and did not straggle or lag behind, and at all times remained and worked in close liaison with the Senior Officer Escort (SOE). Brundle would unfurl as the Commodore's badge the broad St Andrew pennant on *Harmatris*.

The convoy sailed on 28 December from Loch Ewe, and anchored off Reykjavik at Hvalfiordur at 8.20pm on 1 January 1942. Once more Brundle was appointed Commodore, this time for the next stage of the voyage to Russia.

Meanwhile, the escorts were assembling: the Halcyon Class fleet minesweepers *Harrier* (Lieutenant Commander E.P. Hinton) and *Speedwell* (Lieutenant Commander Youngs). As they sailed, *Harrier* was the lead ship, followed by a light cruiser, HMS *Trinidad* (Captain L.S. Saunders), with two Tribal Class destroyers, *Matabele* (Commander Stanford) and *Somali* (Captain Bain – the convoy escort commander), on either side, and with HMS *Speedwell* astern.

The entire convoy sailed out of Hvalfiordur on 8 January 1942 in line abreast, with *Harmatris* as lead merchant ship, and with escorts disposed as described. For two days of this next part of the voyage the strong winds that had blown on the journey to Iceland did not relent.

The convoy left Iceland with a splendid flourish. There was a honking of horns, and signals flashed from one ship to another. Aldis lamps blinked, and a flag signal was hoisted on *Trinidad*, 'Take up your station'. Finally, came the ultimate signal for those under starter's orders, 'Full speed ahead. Maintain your distance.' Each ship took up her place in the small convoy. In *Harmatris* a member of the steward's team brought up to the bridge a steaming mug of coffee for Captain Brundle, who, as Commodore, was casting a proprietary eye on the cluster of ships in the convoy.

There was new hope ahead. The last convoy had been abortive and the fire had burnt itself into Brundle's consciousness, a shocking interlude during which they fought for their lives, and for the life of the ship. This time the convoy would go through, and the cargoes of essential materials would get to Russia. They were in it now, all the way to Murmansk.

Encountering the ice field

The following day the convoy reached a position of 73 degrees 45 minutes north, when it encountered the icefield. Brundle was constrained to alter course. It was dangerous to go too near the ice unless under extreme duress; but now was not the time to take such risks.

You could tell a ship in a convoy was approaching the icefield, or icepack, by something that was called 'ice blink', a condition induced by bright sunlight reflecting off the ice, making the task of lookouts anything from uncomfortable to impossible.

The nearness of the icepack was also indicated by a rapid and sudden fall in temperature. It was prudent to keep well away from the edge of the icepack. Brundle was forced to turn south 20 miles away from the start of it. Sometimes a ship entered the icefield to give a U-boat the slip. This was the case with the merchant ships that used the icepack as a refuge after the in-famous signal to scatter the convoy in PQ-17. In this case the ice was prone to close up behind the ship leaving her becalmed, stranded and entirely imprisoned by the ice, like the ships of the Franklin Expedition. Contrary to this, more prudent ships' Masters would even use light signals to prevent their ships from risking that grinding collision with the ice. To go near the icepack might save a ship, but it most likely brought ruin. It was a last-chance expedient.

Clearing the ice from the ship

There was also the fear that, too near the edge of the icefield, heavy accretions of ice and snow would accumulate and build up on the ship's structure. Once there, the ice would increase in weight, and the increase would be rapid. A few months into the future, in March 1942, a ship in the convoy PQ-12, the whaler *Shera*, had capsized in a heavy swell through being thrust too near the icepack, with the result that heavy ice had built up on her superstructure.

All hands on *Harmatris* and on the other merchant ships would be set to work with picks and shovels chipping away at the ice and clearing away the snow. The Petty Officer in charge of the six naval DEMS gunners on board *Harmatris* would give orders and instructions about keeping the ship's fitted guns ice-free. They were covered up, quilted and jacketed, and steam-heating was played on them. As we shall see, air attack was increasingly a real possibility, and the movement south and the consequent change of course to avoid the icepack exposed the convoy to the likelihood of air attack from Norwegian and Finnish airfields nearby. The crew of all ships would notice proximity to the ice-pack by the lingering and tell-tale presence of a film of ice on the insides of the bulkheads of living spaces.

Twenty-four-hour darkness: the valley of the shadow

Another thing Brundle and the other seamen had to get used to was the unchanging gloom. Morning had a kind of twilight feel to it that, by early afternoon, had become black night, and this lasted until the middle of the next morning. A bonus now, after three days of stormy weather, was gentler conditions. The seas were not as rough although the numbing cold remained appalling.

Harmatris and her crew

Harmatris was 5,395 GRT (gross registered tons). She was an average ship among the tramp steamers of those days taking part in Russian and Atlantic convoys (and *Harmatris* had already had experience of Atlantic convoys). With an enormous carrying capacity, she was well armed too, and among her crew of forty-six were seven DEMS gunners to operate and man the guns. On the ship's poop was a 4-inch low-angle gun, a

20-mm Hispano cannon, five Lewis machine-guns and two twin Marlins. *Harmatris* was loaded up with 8,000 tons of military stores, including tanks, military vehicles, cordite and small-arms ammunition.

The average age of the forty-six members of the crew was 36, Brundle was 47, and there were one or two 'old-timers' older than he. There were also cadets or apprentices on board in their mid-to-late teens who were learning to be officers and imbibing enough seamanship and know-how to be able to take their various officers' 'tickets' in due course. In their mid-teens also were the steward's boy and the galley boy.

Boys at sea

The youngest British combatant killed in the Second World War, as well as being the youngest fatal casualty on the convoys, was the merchant seaman Galley Boy R.V. Steed, who was believed to be 14 years of age when his ship struck a mine in 1943 and he was killed. They were too young to know what life was about, boys like him: evidently they were not too young to die. The war the convoys knew cast its net widely and indiscriminately. A ship was a little floating community of young and old, including, sometimes, the very young and those much older, prematurely launched boys and pensioners recalled to the colours.

On the edge of Murmansk there is a lonely and windswept cemetery, one part of which contains the graves of allied seamen, among whom are a number of these teenagers, drowned at sea, just before reaching the dubious dark haven of Murmansk, or blown up at one of the berths by the predatory Luftwaffe. They were a part of a family from one of the British ports, with seafaring in their blood, who said 'goodbye' to their families and departed with high hopes on the great adventure that led to death in Murmansk, and a lonely grave far from home.

Lascars in the engine-room: stokers and Somalis

There was also a Somali or two among engine-room crew, fire-men or trimmers. The 'donkeyman', as he was called, supervised the work of the firemen or trimmers and engine-room ratings. The trimmers supplied coal to the firemen who stoked the fires. The Somalis came from a long-established seafaring community in South Shields or Cardiff. The ships were well bunkered with sufficient coal to last the entire journey.

Somalis worked as stokers, donkeymen, or firemen. They spoke eloquently in the tales they told among their community of the necessity of keeping the supply of coal moving to the stoke hole, and of keeping the coal in the fire during periods, for example, of bad weather, or when the convoy was under attack. If water was slopping everywhere, it was crucial to have dry coal. The presence of the stoker – and Somalis were good stokers – feeding the boiler enabled the ship to manoeuvre. Hidden away in the ship's engine-room, the Somali stoker, or donkey-man, did his job and gave satisfaction. The colourfully named donkeyman was an important figure. Former Somali stokers spoke of how they were so busy during periods of attack and periods of excessive vigilance that they hadn't time to eat. They kept the crucial fires alive, these Somalis, and tragically, many of them went down, tending their fires, with their fires, into the depths of the ocean.

Clear stars and Bear Island

In the Stygian gloom of an Arctic winter the stars stood out clearly and positively, so that astro-navigation came into play. This was Brundle's strong point. I recall him in the post-war period in Driffield coaching cadets from Hull Trinity House in navigation with the kitchen table covered with protractors, set square, stacks of graph paper and logarithm tables. The proximity of the icepack meant that, along with the fierce and unrelenting cold, there was this phenomenal all-round visibility.

There was a lonely rocky island, Bear Island, well known to peacetime trawler crews, which the convoy had to pass south of to avoid pack ice, and thereafter Jan Mayen Island, another lonely outcrop of rock that functioned merely as a signpost. And all this time there was continual exposure to the German airfields in Norway.

After a week without incident and as the North Cape was passed, hopes were high that the Kola inlet would be reached without distraction. Brundle arranged the ships in single line ahead as a preparation for picking up the pilots to take them into the Kola inlet early the next morning.

Approaching the Kola inlet

Brundle led the convoy at 8 knots on the afternoon of Saturday, 17 January. Zigzagging ahead was the minesweeper *Harrier*. To starboard was *Trinidad*, the light cruiser, while *Matabele* and *Somali* kept station on either side of the convoy, on either beam.

No Russian minesweepers or, indeed, Russian vessels were in evidence, no help of any kind forthcoming from that quarter. Word had been passed that timely assistance to get to the Kola inlet would be provided by the British minesweepers based on the inlet. *Sharpshooter* had already sailed to assist the convoy. HMS *Britomart* and *Salamander* were stuck in the Kola inlet, because of dense fog and nil visibility.

A convoy's commodore was prone to suffer from lack of sleep. There was the anxiety of ensuring that every merchant vessel kept station, that there may be U-boats lurking on the approaches to the Kola inlet, that the men on board were up to scratch and doing their job, that that little cadet on one's own ship, for all his boyish bravado, seemed lonely, anxious, and aloof. All these and a hundred other concerns plucked at Brundle's mind and heart.

That is why, when Robert Brundle saw the ships all in their places in convoy PQ-8, escorts and merchant vessels alike, he experienced a sudden surge of fatigue. So he told the Chief Officer, who was on the bridge, he was going to turn in for some sleep, and he went to his cabin.

Torpedo attack

He had barely put his foot over the threshold when he felt the ship shudder and lift. A violent explosion flung him against his wardrobe, giving him in days to come an almost permanent bruise. A U-boat! Rushing back onto the bridge, he found that Mr Masterman had ordered the engines stopped. No. 1 hold had been struck by two torpedoes. The Chief Officer reported what he had seen, hatches and derricks hurled into the sky. Brundle ordered the lifeboats to be lowered but to remain unlaunched and alongside the ship, and the crew to stand by the lifeboats, and went through the ship with the Chief Officer to inspect the damage.

A cursory inspection revealed a forecastle deck that was a shambles, and a great hole in the starboard side of *Harmatris* below the waterline. The torpedoes had penetrated by the fore-peak and No. 1 hold. The ship began to settle by the head.

So all the crew stood and waited, while Brundle also ordered 'Chippy', the ship's carpenter, to sound the bilges; that is, to measure the level of water rising up in the damaged vessel. The water in the bilges measured 18 inches. 'Chippy' went on taking more soundings, as all waited, only to hear a third explosion, a torpedo, sent into the port side of *Harmatris*.

This time, Brundle felt, they must abandon ship, before lives were lost. Signalling to HMS *Speedwell* by torch, and asking the escort to come alongside, the crew of *Harmatris* pulled towards *Speedwell*, and boarding her, spent the rest of that night of the torpedoes on board. Meanwhile, HMS *Matabele* and *Somali* carried out a patterned depth-charge search for submarines, while that night *Speedwell* circled round *Harmatris*, which was listing far down by the head, with her propeller right out of the water.

The one who fired those torpedoes was the captain of a Type VIIC U-boat lurking at the entrance to the Kola inlet, *U-454*, Kapitänleutnant Burkhard Hackländer.

U-454 and Burkhard Hackländer

Hackländer's was one of a group of three U-boats, the so-called Ulan group, the first U-boat wolfpack to be deployed against Arctic convoys. The first two torpedoes fired by *U-454* were fired from a position on the starboard bow of the convoy, striking *Harmatris* in her No. 1 hold.

While the crew were at their lifeboat stations Brundle and Masterman surveyed the damage. On board *Harmatris* there was a big package of clothing intended for Poles interned in Russia.

This package had been blown open, with the result that the clothes lay hanging from the forward rigging.

No. 1 hold of *Harmatris* also contained some torpedo warheads in its cargo. By great good fortune these had fallen undetonated through the hole in the bottom of the ship.

The escort ships believed that *Harmatris* had hit a mine, although HMS *Matabele* made a report that she had heard a torpedo noise on her hydrophone. And then Hackländer put another torpedo into the port side of *Harmatris*. This had failed to detonate, although this was not appreciated at the time, and it caused a tremor which made Brundle think that he had hit a mine. However, the emergency was enough for him to request help from *Speedwell*. Had the torpedo detonated, even more damage to the ship would have been caused, and possibly some loss of life. For one thing the torpedo warheads that fell out through the hole in the ship would all have gone up and exploded. As it was, the damage was still considerable

Hackländer, the commander of *U-454*, although *Harmatris* obstinately refused to sink, was to make an attack on one of the escorts and achieve success. We will come to this later. For the moment it must be said that the U-boat campaign, both in the Atlantic and in the Arctic, caused destruction of allied shipping on a massive scale. Conversely, the U-boat offensive took its own toll of casualties among the U-boat men who, among all Second-World-War combatants, had not much going for them in the survival stakes. The U-boat memorial near Kiel records the names of 27,491 men who died, of 39,000 who went to sea in U-boats.

Hackländer was indeed fortunate, as a member of the U-boat arm, to survive the war. He was sunk on 1 August 1943 by an RAF Sunderland of 10 RAAF Squadron of Coastal Command in the Bay of Biscay. *U-454*'s gunners sold their lives dearly on this encounter, blazing away relentlessly with their returning fire. And so the U-boat was sunk, and the Sunderland crashed into the sea, with only six of the crew of twelve able to be rescued, and with the pilot, Flight Lieutenant K.G. Fry, losing his life. Hackländer and twelve of his U-boat crew were picked up by the Royal Navy, and became prisoners of war. The rest of the crew of *U-454* perished.

We turn from Hackländer and his capture in the Bay of Biscay to *Harmatris*, the ship he attacked on that Arctic night on 17 January 1942. The crew of *Harmatris* were evacuated and transferred on board HMS *Speedwell*, the minesweeper that stayed close to *Harmatris* all that night.

After three torpedo hits Brundle expected his ship to sink, and he was not the only one. He reflected that at least, on his ship, no lives had been lost. But, as he looked, from the deck of *Speedwell*, at *Harmatris*, listing far down by the head, with her propeller right out of the water, he came increasingly to feel that the ship and the valuable cargo, after the 2,000-mile journey to Russia, could be, ought to be saved. It would be a great pity and disappointment to abandon 8,000 tons of crucial war material to the great deep of the Arctic Ocean, now that they were so close to the Kola inlet and to Murmansk. Meanwhile, the vice commodore aboard the American vessel *Larranga* escorted the convoy past the stricken *Harmatris*.

Harmatris is towed by *Speedwell*

Brundle, in between his reflections in the small hours and making sure his men were not injured after the events of the night, asked the captain of *Speedwell*, Lieutenant Commander Youngs, if he would take *Harmatris* in tow, and tow her to port. Youngs agreed after some persuasion. It certainly needed thinking about. To tow would make you, as well as the ship you towed, a slow-moving and vulnerable target for torpedoes, and possibly a prey to enemy aircraft from the Finnish and Norwegian coast. But after some persuasion the captain of *Speedwell* agreed. It had been hammered into them during convoy conferences and preparations for sailing just how valuable, crucial even, were the cargoes of these early convoys. Russia, with the Nazis outside Moscow and the beginning of the terrible siege of Leningrad, had her back to the wall. She and Britain were the only powers not overrun by Hitler. Britain had won her strategically important Battle of Britain, with the RAF playing a significant role, in 1940, and Russia from June 1941 was fighting for her life. The sinking of 8,000 tons of war material created a sufficient dent in Russian needs and expectation, to make it, at this time and moment in history, of supreme importance. So the preparations for *Harmatris* to be towed by *Speedwell* began. The convoy escort commander was consulted, and the decision was made.

Brundle mustered his men, on board *Speedwell*, and asked for volunteers to re-board *Harmatris* and man her during the towing operation. It was too dangerous a projected action to give the order to re-board. It was a matter for volunteers. To Brundle's surprise and pleasure, everyone of the crew of *Harmatris* stepped forward. Without further ado they were conveyed back on board, and the towing sweeps were connected.

Soon after starting the towing, however, the towing sweeps broke. On investigation it was found that the starboard anchor had been let go by the force of the first explosion, and was dragging along the sea bed in ninety fathoms of water. The windlass also had been shattered by the same explosion. So the anchor could not be raised at all. It would not budge.

The job would need to be done manually, by brute force. Hammers and punches were sent for, and the men began splitting the cable.

Meanwhile, after this attack on *Harmatris*, the convoy had scattered. Escort vessels from the Royal Navy circled and zig-zagged around the merchant ships like worried sheepdogs, and the seven merchant vessels formed up in line ahead, having resumed their original course at 8 knots.

At 9.45pm HMS *Sharpshooter* joined the escorts of the convoy. She was based in the Kola inlet. This ship, *Sharpshooter*, like those other Halcyon Class minesweepers, *Harrier* and *Speedwell*, which helped PQ-8 considerably on the approaches to the Kola inlet, were all members of the 6th Minesweeping Flotilla, based in the Kola inlet, and from that base ready to provide close escort for incoming convoys. For the convoys themselves the final run, the approach to Russian waters and the Kola inlet was regarded as the most dangerous part of the entire convoy. That was when submarines, lurking in the vicinity of Kildin Island, often made their attack. That, after all, is where Hackländer attacked *Harmatris*.

There developed the practice that minesweepers of the Halcyon class would sail with the outward convoy, as 'through' escorts, and then, as *Harrier* and *Speedwell* did, stay in Russian waters to give 'close' escort, sweeping and clearing mines ahead of the homeward-bound convoys. Their duties also included meeting and escorting the inward-bound convoys. In the spring it was home to Britain. Operating this in strict rotation they were usually relieved at the end of their period of duty. As one Able Seaman noted in his diary, 'Eight months in this joint is enough to drive anyone screwy'. The captain and crew of *Harmatris* would be in a position later on to endorse this opinion wholeheartedly and with feeling.

Sharpshooter had been trying to reach PQ-8 for some time, but severe fog had frustrated her progress. On arrival she stationed herself on the starboard beam of the convoy. HMS *Matabele*, which had originally been instructed to drop back and assist *Harmatris*, and finding that her assistance was not now required, rejoined the convoy and its screen of escorts at 10.15pm, and took up a position to starboard.

Matabele is sunk

The convoy could by now see the flashing lighthouse beam on the Kola inlet from Cape Teriberski, 10 miles away. This, tragically, served to illuminate the ships of the convoy for Burkhard Hackländer of *U-454*, the same U-boat commander who had put three torpedoes into *Harmatris*. This time Hackländer had the tanker *British Pride* in his sights. Manoeuvring his boat into position, he loosed off a fan of torpedoes. These missed the tanker but struck HMS *Matabele*, like *Somali*, one of the Tribal Class destroyers in PQ-8's escort, in her magazine.

Matabele went up with a coruscating flash. Only two survivors, Ordinary Seamen Higgins and Burras, were picked up, and 217 members of the crew perished. Most of those who died were killed by the Arctic cold of the sea. For those in the water, waiting to be picked up, the freezing cold would drive the air from the lungs in a second. That is a terrific shock to the system. After this they would go down into the dark waters, numbingly cold and very quiet. Most had no option but to surrender. Equally most, having advertised their presence by shouting and screaming, so that the rescue boats would know their location, were unable, with no air in their lungs, to shout any more. So, in the end, there was little panic or motion or struggle, when the drowning came.

The third of the three torpedoes Hackländer fired struck *Matabele* between her two funnels, squarely amidships. To those on board her it seemed as if she was being lifted out of the water. There was then a violent listing of the ship, which was only momentary. The ship picked up from this, and righted herself.

Fire now began to spread alarmingly. Cries came from men in the water. Fire cut off little parties of men. Some men became trapped in jammed bulkheads, and steel rooms, and their cries could be heard. Death found crewmen in many different ways, in spite of escape and survival modes and techniques they had learned in the classroom, sleepy, bored and docile before the blackboard.

When the torpedo hit, one of the ship's gunners, Ordinary Seaman Ernest Higgins, under instruction from the first lieutenant of HMS *Matabele*, began to close all magazine accesses on the after deck. As he saw his comrades in the water he desperately tried to free the Carley floats, but they were frozen, and hammering and chipping away would not free them. Being ordered to go to the foredeck similarly to close those magazine hatches, Higgins and others were brought up short by the explosion, a blast and a sheet of flame, as *Matabele*'s main magazine emptied and blew up.

The destroyer, the proud *Matabele*, was by now ripped in two. Bow and stern had parted from each other and pointed, almost in mocking fashion, at the sky. Higgins was scared to jump. The prospect appalled him, but he had to go, over the side and into the water. Instinctively he tightened his life jacket around him, pulling at the tapes and making it tight. All round Higgins, when he entered the water, were fellow ratings, swimming desperately in the freezing water, striking out boldly, so that they would not become victims of the sunken vessel's terrible displacement when the two parts entered the troubled deep. To Higgins it seemed unlikely that rescue in this freezing Arctic water would come in time. It was at this point that it would have been easy, painfully, fatally easy to surrender to the overwhelming cold, and simply sink beneath the waves. Others were doing it. Others were screaming in the water, seeking to attract the attention of potential rescuers. It was a nightmare scene. What seamen feared, when they were tossing and turning in bunks and hammocks, had come to pass.

Just then Higgins saw something in the water. It looked like a piece of wreckage. It was in fact a boarding net, magnificently coiled up, and of enough bulk to offer desperate men some kind of sanctuary from the ocean and the cruel, bitter cold. Higgins called to a man he saw next to him in the water. It was another of the gun team of 'X' turret, Ordinary Seaman William Burras. Both men, Higgins and Burras, swam towards the net. It was, at the time, their only hope. Before they were picked up, they had sunk into a state of semi-consciousness. They were covered in thick, crude oil that caked the surface of the sea in which they found themselves.

Paradoxically, though the oil could have choked them, it most likely formed a protection for them from the icy cold.

Somali, meanwhile, while these momentous things were happening, was on the other side of the convoy. Those on her deck saw the distress rockets of *Matabele* arch into the blackness of the night sky. Increasing her speed to 20 knots, *Somali* hastened up as support. She had just crossed the bows of the tanker *British Pride*, when the massive explosion was heard, indicating that *Matabele*'s magazine had gone up.

It was now futile for Captain Bain of *Somali*, who was Senior Escort Commander, to go to *Matabele*'s aid. He ordered HMS *Harrier* to stand by *Matabele*, while he himself sailed in a wide sweep as much as 10 miles to starboard of the convoy, firing star shells and probing for Asdic contacts. Obviously there was a U-boat there, and several positive Asdic contacts were made. A depth-charge attack followed, but without result.

Hackländer had gone deep, was lying, in fact, almost on the bottom, while the depth-charges exploded harmlessly above him. When the depth-charge attack was suspended, he was off and away. When *Harrier* appeared on the scene, *Matabele* had sunk and many men had gone under the water. The destroyer's total complement when she had set off in the escorts from Iceland was 219. Two ordinary seamen, Ernest Higgins and William Burras, were the only ones *Harrier* was able to pull out alive from the sea. Later, the body of Lieutenant Commander E.J.T. Winn was found. As one writer expresses it, it was as if the 'honeymoon' period of the Russian convoys was well and truly over. From now on casualties would proliferate, ships would go down, and the scale of things pointed over the horizon to aircraft carriers, cruisers, frigates and untold destroyers and minesweepers all making the 'suicide run' (as Royal and Merchant Navy personnel who travelled on it called it) to Russia.

It was in vain that *Harrier* put out the nets over her sides to scoop up the odd survivor. There was no one who could or would respond. The entire ship's company of *Matabele* had been swallowed up, apart from the two survivors mentioned. It was a startling reminder of the cost of bringing munitions, food, and military equipment to North Russia. Escorts, as well as merchant ships, were intensely vulnerable. Death did not make any distinction between those who flew the Red Duster and those who flew the White Ensign. It could touch them all. The naval escorts were the protectors of the merchant ships; but death, nothing if not impartial, reached out her hand to both.

The sinking of HMS *Matabele* and the tremendous loss of life sustained was deeply felt. As already indicated, PQ-8 was a watershed in the Russian convoy system, portending the shape of things to come. From now on, losses of ships and personnel, both merchantmen and Royal Navy, were frequent on the Russian run.

The struggle on *Harmatris* to splice the anchor cable

On the deck of *Harmatris* the struggle went on to splice the anchor cable. The job was almost impossible, and the icy weather made the job doubly difficult. *Speedwell*'s captain, Lieutenant Commander Youngs, signalled to Robert Brundle that he and his crew would be less vulnerable on *Speedwell* than in a highly exposed position on *Harmatris*. The fate of *Matabele* was so fresh and such an overwhelming shock, the sights and sounds from all those drowning bodies, the smell of the oil slick, and the flotsam and debris of a mighty destroyer, swallowed up in an instant by disaster.

Thus Brundle and his crew yet again spent a night on *Speedwell*. The stay was only a brief overnight one. At 6.00am the next morning it was back to *Harmatris* for the whole crew, there to find that the steam pipes on deck were frozen solid. By an oversight the main steam had been left on all night, and the boilers had run dry. Ordinary aids were therefore unworkable and inoperable. No winches could be employed. The cable had to be split by sheer, manual brute force.

Eventually, with much toil and effort, and exercise of manual strength, the cable was cut, and sweeps were attached to the bollards of *Harmatris*. The towing began, with the two ships sailing their own lonely course. The rest of the convoy had preceded them and sailed on.

The shock of the loss of *Matabele* remained with the men of *Harmatris*, whom she had been escorting, for a long time. In the short term it reinforced and underlaid the sweat and toil expended in the towing operation. But the shock bore heavily too on the men of all the escort vessels, especially on the men of her 'chummy ship', her sister Tribal Class destroyer, HMS *Somali*, for they knew some of the men who had gone down with *Matabele*, and the crew must have wondered if they would be the next U-boat victim.

Enemy airfields

Uncomfortably near, in terms of flying time, to the Russian ports towards which PQ-8 was sailing, were enemy airfields. These were Bardufoss, Banak, Tromso and Narvik in Norway, as well as the Finnish airbase of Petsamo, which fielded 230 aircraft in all, to be deployed on the Arctic front. In later times in the convoy story, at the time of the September 1942 homeward convoy, for example, QP-14, the long-range Blohm und Voss BV 138 reconnaissance flying boat had constantly shadowed the convoy. They had only to radio for torpedo-carrying Heinkel He 111 or Junkers Ju 87 and Ju 88 bombers and they would be down on a convoy in an instant. No doubt, in the case of PQ-8 approaching the Kola inlet, *U-454*, which had wreaked such havoc in the convoy, communicated the presence and location of PQ-8's ships.

In Norway at Banak, Major Bloedorn's Kampfgeschwader 30 had Junkers Ju 88 dive-bombers, and at Bardufoss, also in Norway, Colonel Roth's KG 26 had Heinkel He 111 torpedo-bombers. It was the custom to attack with both aircraft types together, particularly using Junkers Ju 88s and Heinkel He 111s for convoy work.

Air attack on *Harmatris* and *Speedwell*

There was one more hazard in the chain of perils and calamities for *Speedwell* and *Harmatris* to face before they arrived at their destination. On the morning of 18 January, while *Harmatris* was being towed towards the Kola inlet, and during the brief envelope of dark twilight, as bright as it gets in the unending period of dark days of an Arctic winter, an He 111 swooped in on *Harmatris* at almost mast-top height, spraying the ship with cannon and machine-gun fire.

Harmatris had seven able DEMS gunners on board, trained RN ratings under the command of a PO gunner. They were at action stations, and in conjunction with *Speedwell* and her guns, returned the Heinkel's fire, and drove it off with several hits.

Defensively Equipped Merchant Ships

The presence of these DEMS gunners on board a merchant ship was a great boon to the defence and security of the ship, and they gave a good account of themselves in the incident I am recounting. In the opening phase of the war it was a struggle to process and dispatch to their parent ships these naval gunners, and recourse was made to the training-up of merchant navy personnel in gunnery skills. Some 1,500 merchant navy personnel therefore received gunnery training during the first full year of war. As the war went on and the scheme for DEMS gunners was seen to work well, their number was supplemented, with those who were available for this, Army gunners, of whom 14,000 served in this capacity, and of whom 1,222 made the supreme sacrifice. As it was, some 24,000 RN DEMS gunners served on board merchant ships, of whom about 5,000 were killed. Like the gunners in an RAF bomber, DEMS gunmen were frequently in action, and the fact that just over a quarter of them were killed in action is testimony to their presence in the front line, where the action was hottest.

A special feature, 'A Seaman Gunner Arrives', from my grandfather's memorabilia, is in my possession as part of *Neptune*, the Merchant Navy Magazine for Merchant Seamen for July 1943 (No. 40). The article shows the newly trained gunner arriving at his ship, and then backtracks to his training, including aircraft recognition, practice at the sights of a Bofors gun, and training with the 12-pounder anti-aircraft gun. In one picture, showing the rating training on the 12-pounder, there is a typical intrusive message, plastered across the photograph, that reminds me that I am holding in my hand a contemporary historical document. There is a hand pointing to the young trainees, and a message above it, which says: 'You can hit back with your savings too!' – an item as lively and historically contemporary as the one at the foot of the last paragraph in the magazine: 'When you have read this magazine, pass it on.'

The magazine is printed in four languages, the four Merchant Navy languages current at the time: English, French, Norwegian and Dutch, the languages of England and of the prime three free navies. The same issue of *Neptune* contains, in comic-strip form, an account of this voyage of *Harmatris* in PQ-8.

PAC Rockets and a Ju 88

Brundle, meanwhile, during this aerial attack attempted to release the PAC (Parachute and Cable) rockets *Harmatris* carried, but to no avail, as they were all frozen. The PAC rockets released at speed into the air projectiles that fluttered down slowly from height with trailing cables, which were sometimes sufficient to ensnare and tangle up low-flying aircraft as they made their low passes over our ships. But they failed, impossibly frozen, because of the low temperatures.

But if the PAC rockets didn't work, the guns did, and our tracer was observed hitting the aircraft, which was last seen disappearing over land on the port bow of *Harmatris*, with a dense plume of smoke billowing out from it.

A second enemy aircraft, a Junkers Ju 88, mounted an additional attack an hour later, manoeuvring itself into a good position for the assault. The crew of *Harmatris*, at action stations throughout, saw bombs dropped on the port and starboard sides. As they dropped from the bomb bay of the aircraft, each one looked as though it had your name on it, as if the bombs were coming straight towards you. To the deep relief of the crew of *Harmatris* all the bombs were wide of the mark. As they crashed into the sea, they threw up jets of water in the shape of tall plumes, drenching with their spray the crewmen of *Harmatris*, who had thrown themselves flat on the decks. A direct hit would have annihilated most of the crew. But not a man was injured or lost. As for the machine-gun fire, the bullets had 'pinged' off iron rails and stanchions. Bullet holes were discovered in the ship's bulwarks and ventilators. One bullet passed through the captain's sitting room, another through the Chief Officer's room.

Seafarers, on average, are more religious than the next man, and certainly more superstitious. Brundle noticed not a few on their knees and praying (something he told me about a few times) as the second aircraft disappeared over land on the starboard side, like the first, having taken several hits and with smoke pouring from it. The consistent firepower of *Harmatris* and *Speedwell* had driven off the two enemy aircraft at the most vulnerable time for the two ships, when they must have been sitting ducks. Later, in Murmansk, when Brundle happened to meet Lieutenant Commander Youngs of *Speedwell*, he informed him that the first enemy aircraft to attack had been brought down, and that the Russians had given credit for bringing it down to both *Harmatris* and *Speedwell*, while the other aircraft, although badly damaged, made good its escape.

Enemy aircraft detached from a Murmansk bombing raid to attack *Harmatris*?

When a concerted attack was made on a convoy, and this happened in the case of some of the later convoys, so many Ju 88 dive-bombers were called up from Banak and so many He 111 torpedo-bombers from Bardufoss and they would mount a co-ordinated attack on the ships, employing bombs and torpedoes.

It looked very much as if the two aircraft that attacked *Harmatris* and *Speedwell* had been detached from a larger bombing raid on Murmansk or some of the Kola inlet ports, given that the two ships attacked were only 8 miles from Cape Teriberski and the entrance to the Kola inlet. It would have been a terrible outcome had the He 111 been able to let loose a torpedo against *Harmatris* or *Speedwell*. At that point of towing, they were in an extremely vulnerable position. Fortunately for the two ships, the first enemy aircraft, before he tried a torpedo attack, came over mast-high with a low-level attack, spraying bullets indiscriminately. The aircraft then was caught up in the concerted and co-ordinated firepower of the AA guns of *Speedwell* and of the seven DEMS gunners of *Harmatris*. Both crews observed bullets striking the aircraft. Black smoke was seen pouring out of it as it passed low and landwards, and in Murmansk Brundle was told it had crashed. This must have acted as a deterrent to the Junkers Ju 88 following, as, after one brief machine-gun and bomb attack it had had enough and it had been hit several times. Its bombs were wide of the mark. The DEMS crew of *Harmatris* had demon-strated their worth and their skills supremely in the teeth of a tricky and menacing sudden attack. It could have so easily gone the other way. Instead the exercise of their firepower had crippled the He 111 so much that it could not go round and re-emerge for what would have been a fatal torpedo attack. The guns of the two ships had driven the aircraft off, and so disabled it that it crashed on land, with a deterrent effect on the second aircraft.

After the attack by two enemy aircraft, but with the men in correspondingly good heart, the towing proceeded apace. Eventually a tug came out from Teriberski Bay to take over the towing of *Harmatris*. The faithful *Speedwell*, which had guarded *Harmatris* so constantly and vigilantly and had towed her through the recent deadly assault had now to part company with her, as three members of her crew had been badly scalded when a steam pipe had burst at high pressure in her boiler room. She had to make for Murmansk with all speed to succour her wounded. Brundle, appreciating the assistance Lieutenant Commander Youngs of *Speedwell* had given him during the last two days of this extraordinary and eventful voyage, wrote in his report, after arriving in Murmansk with the propeller of *Harmatris* exposed and out of the water:

> *We arrived off this port* [Murmansk] *on the 20th and berthed at 2.00pm local time. The old 'Red Duster' still flies over this ship, and, once again Britain has delivered the goods. In conclusion I must say that I am delighted with the hospitality shown to my officers and crew and myself by all members of HMS* Speedwell. *I think they are wonderful, and it is nice to see such co-operation between the two services. Long may it reign.*

Harmatris reaches Murmansk

The absence of *Speedwell*, which had engendered such bonds of gratitude and affection in the captain and crew of *Harmatris*, was made up for by a Russian tug. Another two tugs joined this one at 5.00pm, and *Harmatris* finally, after enough action for every one of the crew to last a lifetime, berthed at Murmansk (as Brundle said in his report) at 2.00pm on 20 January.

Looking at the vessel with his carpenter and engineers, Brundle could see that all iron locking bars had been blown away. Missing were wood hatches and tarpaulins. The five iron beams were strewn about the decks, and odd fragments of cargo, in all the multiple explosions, had become entwined among the rigging. The whole thing looked like a dirty, hastily decorated Christmas tree.

There was water everywhere, three parts in No. 1 hold. The bulkhead forward had been badly fractured. So also the fore peak tank and the fore and aft bulkhead. And yet they had reached Murmansk with their cargo and their lives, and their overriding feeling was one of intense relief. The Russians, it must be said, however, were not geared up and ready for all the materials and cargo they would receive from incoming convoys. The two tankers in PQ-8, *British Pride* and *British Workman*, were both full of aviation spirit, a vital commodity, especially for Murmansk, with all the bombing, and a number of boxed Hurricanes needing to be assembled and needing fuel. And yet they discharged their cargo directly into railway wagons immediately onto the jetty, which lacked all other facilities, a risky option, especially while bombing raids were going on. Proper facilities for discharge were almost completely lacking anywhere in Murmansk. For those ships entering harbour after the trials of the journey to Russia, disillusionment set in.

It was to be a long time before *Harmatris*, whose appearance told her own story, would be ready for sailing again. Months of frustration, her next set of trials, lay ahead.

CHAPTER 6

Murmansk and Archangel: Bombing and Food Shortages

Whatever people may tell him [the man in the street] *the bomber will always get through.*

Stanley Baldwin, 1932

Hunger allows no choice to the citizen or the police;
We must love one another, or die.

W.H. Auden: 'Hunger allows
no choice', 1939

Murmansk, 'the land on the sea shore', or 'the land on the edge of the world', in the Sami language of Russian Lapland, was a sea port on the Kola inlet. In First-World-War times it was never more than a collection of shacks, and, although much improved since those days, it had a kind of provisional nature about it, as if you wouldn't see it tomorrow, like something out of *The Wizard of Oz*, and certainly its reputation during the war as the most bombed Soviet city after Stalingrad made the eventuality increasingly likely.

Strategic importance of Murmansk

After the end of the First World War Murmansk was the scene
of fighting between the Bolsheviks and a force of allies from
the Western powers, who tried, with White Russians, to over-
throw the revolutionary forces. The expedition foundered on
the political support given to these western interventionists. So
Murmansk was no stranger to violence. Its role in what Russians
called the Great Patriotic War made of it the critical link in
the supply chain in north-east Russia, as well as the landfall for
allied convoys.

Murmansk was vital. Immediately before the outbreak of the
war and Germany's invasion of Poland, Stalin sought to protect
the approach by sea to Leningrad and to provide a buffer zone
around Murmansk. Experience in the closing stages of the Russian
Civil War had taught him that Murmansk was a little Achilles'
heel as far as the USSR was concerned. It must be protected at all
costs. So Stalin began what came to be known as the Winter War
with Russia's small neighbour, Finland.

The Winter War

Finland was a tiny nation, on a par with the Baltic states of
Estonia, Latvia and Lithuania, which Stalin, having addressed
with protestations of friendship and co-operation in a common
cause, kept down and subdued by garrisoning there ever-
increasing numbers of troops.

Finland, the David to the USSR's Goliath, was, of course,
eventually overwhelmed, and forced to cede territory to the
Soviets. But the bargaining and the dispositions were not all
one-sided. After all, the Finns had inflicted in the early part of the
Winter War a series of crushing defeats on the Russians, which
resulted in their having lost 200,000 men, 700 aircraft and 1,600
tanks. The Russian Marshal Timoshenko was appointed by Stalin
to re-form and re-energise the Red Army, so that such reverses
suffered against the Finns would never happen again.

There is a port to the west of the Finnish capital, Helsinki,
called Hamko. One of the items to result from the Russian–
Finnish settlement was that this port was leased to the USSR for

a period of thirty years, to become a naval base that would close the Gulf of Finland.

So the Arctic north-east of Russia was written deeply into the history of the USSR as an area of instability. Russian Lapland was Russia's 'Wild West', Russia's badlands. The Germans had plans to walk in there from Norway, but the Finnish settlement precluded that. Sadly Finland, entirely because of her recent history, found herself in the Axis camp; but the truth was rather that she behaved like a neutral state. For example, in August 1941 the Germans asked Mannerheim, the Finnish General, to advance beyond the recovered territory and cut off Leningrad. He refused.

Purge of the Red Army

In the trauma of post-war guilt and blame and counter-blame and accusation Stalin carried out a thoroughgoing purge of the Red Army's officer corps in which 26,671 officers were sacked, imprisoned or executed. Indeed, of 706 officers of brigade commander rank and above only 303 in all remained untouched. In view of subsequent history, and Nazi Germany's invasion of Russia on 22 June 1941, this left the USSR fatally weakened. Tragically and catastrophically Marshal Mikhail Tukhachevsky was the most senior victim of the purge.

He was the Rommel and the Guderian of the Red Army, the leading Russian advocate of mobile warfare, of blitzkrieg Russian-style, and the army was immeasurably the poorer for his passing and the demise of all those gifted officers. Hitler frustrated the purposes of his senior generals, and admirals and air marshals, and overruled them constantly. Stalin did this, but he executed them as well.

Given the state of the Soviet army after these purges, it is a wonder they rallied, made the progress they did and achieved the victory of Stalingrad by early 1943. After the initial and well-known psychological paralysis of Stalin, following the German invasion which lasted for just over a fortnight, a brand-new Russian Stavka (High Command) had been formed. Voroshilov, Timoshenko and Budenny were given joint commands to hold the line. And hold it they did. Churchill referred to 'the Russian people's passionate defence of their native soil'.

Murmansk and the bombers

Murmansk became a symbol of all this. Rising to a height of some 40 metres above the present city is a statue of an unknown soldier, Alyosha. It is not another version of Stalinist brutalism, this colossus in concrete, but a figure who seems to be reflecting sorrowfully as he gazes over the waters where the ships of the convoys came in, and so manages to be an utterly convincing memorial of the desperate things that happened in Murmansk, and of the loss of life sustained by Russians and allied seamen alike.

In 1983 Murmansk was designated as a 'Hero City' by the Soviet government. So British and Russians alike, we are in agreement that momentous things happened here in the Second World War, and that frequent and prolonged attempts to transport military hardware and provisions to this port helped to keep the German invading forces at bay. And yet the city was well-nigh obliterated by German bombers. Ninety-five per cent of Murmansk was razed to the ground.

Murmansk, on the Kola inlet, had suffered since the time of the earliest convoys from bombings. There were few anti-aircraft guns and very few resources and facilities in the port itself. Even the largest crane in Murmansk was incapable of lifting tanks, and the convoy cargoes were full of tanks and other military vehicles. As wants and needs in the ports became increasingly understood, ships with heavy-lifting facilities were sent out with the convoys.

And yet Murmansk was important. For one thing it was ice-free all the year round, the first port of call for most convoys, and the enemy were desperate to capture it. It was the port into which Brundle was towed by Soviet tugs after such a hazardous and memorable journey with PQ-8.

From Murmansk ran the railway line to Leningrad and the line to Moscow. The Nazi armies were outside both these cities. The siege of Leningrad, 900 days of it, in which 1.02 million inhabitants died, was to burn itself into the collective memory of the Russian psyche, while the battle for Moscow in late 1941 was the focus of all Russian resistance.

The Germans cut the line to Leningrad, but the Russians put down new track between Belomorsk and Obuzerskaye to link up with the line from Archangel to Moscow. Murmansk may have been a poor thing, with few berths for the incoming convoys, and with a disconcerting exposure to the Heinkels and Junkers that flew in to bomb from Finland and Norway, but it was, in the Russian north-east, a symbol of resistance alongside Leningrad.

Some ships berthed at the Northern Fleet HQ of the Red Navy at Polyarnoe, which was quite near to the mouth of the Kola inlet. Polyarnoe had the merit of lying in a deep fiord, which was well protected. It, like most of Murmansk, was a bit ramshackle with wooden wharfs, but it suited the purpose of some war-weary convoys at the end of their run, for whom no accommodation could be provided at Murmansk or Archangel for various reasons. Robert Brundle had cause to visit Polyarnoe a number of times.

One other place, on the other side of the Kola inlet from Polyarnoe a few miles north of Murmansk, was a particularly exposed anchorage, Vaenga Bay, and yet it assumed an importance out of all proportion to its bulk and extent. For it was here that ships came with boxed parts of Hurricanes to be unloaded, put together, maintained, tested, and delivered to their fledgling Russian pilots to try out and work up, under the expert guidance of a team of RAF instructors (a dangerous job for them). Vaenga did not look up to the job but it was a hive of activity. Airstrips in nearby pine forests, the classic trees of the Northern Russian taiga, hid boxes and boxes of parts ready for assembling, while at the little wooden wharfs there were corvettes, trawlers, destroyers and cruisers, berthed wherever they could, any port in a storm. The Russian convoy experience, at the other end, was a massive exercise in 'Make do and mend'.

'But the Russians never mended anything', as one naval officer remembered. This was partly true. Certainly this was how it was perceived by allied seamen gazing at all the massive and disappointing neglect and chaos around them, left in the interludes of thrice-daily visits by the Luftwaffe. Certain incomplete parts of *Harmatris* repaired by the Russians had to be done all over again. Standards were, on the whole, poor.

Merchant seamen, cargoes and ship repair

Herein lies the crux of the fate of the merchant seamen during the experiences of the Russian run. The crews of the Royal Navy escort ships were responsible, so the naval code described it, for 'the safe and timely arrival of the convoy'. When this was done, then their job was done. For the merchant seamen, by contrast, arrival at port did not mean a hiatus in their responsibilities. After bringing a full cargo through all the hazards of the run to Murmansk or Archangel, a duty of a most difficult kind waited for them at the end of the process, and that was the discharge of their cargo under prolonged and frequent air attack.

Furthermore, if, as was the case with *Harmatris*, the ship was badly damaged, their captain and crew had to contrive and bring about the repairs and stay with the ships until this was finished, until it was thoroughly seaworthy and ready for a homeward convoy. That, indeed, was why *Harmatris* and crew had an eight-month stay, largely in Murmansk, but latterly in Archangel, while all these goals and objectives were brought about, and during all this time were at the mercy of the thrice-daily bombing, as well as being in the grip of an appalling shortage of food.

Naval representation in North Russian ports

There were two principal naval units in the North Russian ports, NP100, stationed at Murmansk, and NP200, stationed at Archangel. Rear Admiral G.J.A. Miles, who had been head of the British Naval Liaison Mission since 25 June 1941, handled diplomatic issues, while the Senior British Naval Officer, North Russia (SBNONR) was, at first, Rear Admiral R.H. Bevan. He had to liaise with his Russian opposite number, Admiral Golovko, commander of the Soviet Northern Fleet, and deal with issues relating to the convoys, both in relation to naval escorts and merchant ships. We shall see Rear Admiral Bevan intervening when *Harmatris* had to vacate a berth she was promised, and

Bevan had to uphold the cause of a destroyer which needed immediate repair. Miles succeeded Bevan as SBNONR. Other SBNONRs included Rear Admiral E.P. Archer and Rear Admiral J. Edgerton.

It is interesting to reflect that the working instructions for the SBNONR included the destruction of all port facilities and plant in North Russia, if, as seemed likely when the convoys started up, the collapse of Soviet resistance was brought about by the Germans. This sober reflection brings home the truth of how much matters stood on a knife edge. My grandfather and hundreds of seamen in Murmansk and Archangel might then have become prisoners of war. More grievously the disastrous outcome of losing the war might then have been staring the allies in the face.

At Murmansk NP100 and Rear Admiral Bevan handled incoming radio traffic from the convoys and transmitted any decoded enemy signals to the appropriate intelligence network. He organised pre-convoy conferences for the QP- convoys and appointed the commodores and, very importantly, the SBNONR also had control of the Halcyon Class minesweepers, which kept the channels all around the Kola inlet clear of mines and provided a close escort to Murmansk for ships of incoming convoys.

As the time of waiting in Murmansk or Archangel lengthened, the crews struggled to keep their ships free of snow and ice. Sometimes water became rationed. Scabies became a problem. It was hard keeping clean when there was not enough water to wash in, let alone to drink.

One monumental inadequacy in the long litany of laments from the Russian ports already mentioned, as it impinged on the discharge of the cargo of *Harmatris* as soon as port was reached, was the absence of heavy-lifting gear. It was not until April/ May 1942 that heavy-lift ships like *Empire Bard* and *Empire Elgar* reached the North Russian ports. Another element sorely lacking, particularly at Murmansk, was adequate weaponry, particularly anti-aircraft guns to meet the challenge of the German bombers. German bombers, as we shall see, caused a harvest of destruction among ships lying at their berths in Murmansk. With the advent of powerful anti-aircraft weapons, and the training of crews in their use, there was a welcome hiatus in the trail of destruction in Murmansk from June 1942 (a particularly bad month, when Robert Brundle was in the thick of it, and witnessed the loss of a number of ships in this way) to March 1943. Whatever the nature of the bombing, whatever horrors were faced, control was top of the agenda for the Russians.

The Soviet regime was obsessed with passes and permissions. Merchant seamen who arrived in Murmansk as survivors, after fighting every inch of the way to reach it, were left cold and hungry and largely forgotten on the edge of some quay until they were transferred to a holding camp by embarrassed representatives of the MOWT and there given meagre rations until they were shipped back on a homeward-bound convoy.

Wanted – 'Empire' lifting ships

Refugee seamen in Russian ports could not gain information about the progress of the war. Even mail was delayed, and to the absolute disgust of intended recipients, interfered with. Such things lay heavily on crews of the 'Empire' ships with their winches and cranes and heavy-lifting apparatus, who were occupied at the ports as part of an extended duty for anything up to eight or nine months. Their presence and participation was particularly required now that out-of-date Matilda tanks were not much seen in incoming British cargoes, but instead Grant and Churchill tanks, which were twice the weight of the Matildas.

Hospital facilities

For the wounded and the sick, and those tended to come into the ports in ever-increasing numbers, a grim lottery operated. In Murmansk before a bombing raid in June 1942 there was a hospital where staff strove with all might and main, and with completely uncharacteristic self-denial, to provide the basics in cleanliness and care. The only snag was that they were out of anaesthetics. For every story of shortages and neglect, there was an alternative story doing the rounds of amputation, carried out speedily and effectively to prevent the onset of gangrene. Such was the case at Vaenga, a diminutive hospital, where patients were crammed two abed.

At the same time every effort was made to ship needy cases back on return convoys or warships with medical personnel and proper facilities. *Zaafaran* and *Zamalek*, which had sailed in convoy PQ-6, being officially designated as 'rescue ships', were two such ships fitted out with all the facilities, doctors and medical staff included. Sadly the first ship, *Zaafaran* was sunk in PQ-17, with crew and all personnel being rescued by her sister ship.

These features and elements and special circumstances were all a part of the hectic and varied life of the convoy men, both *en route* to Russia, and especially during their enforced sojourn in the North Russian ports. Meanwhile, Russian officials at these ports, impervious to the stresses and strains, the lives swallowed up by the Arctic Ocean and the cost of the Russian run as evinced in other ways (and there was an entire crop of 'unseen' mental casualties, who were permanently impaired), would end a speech of so-called 'welcome' in a manner appropriate to addresses given to rival, competitive labour gangs, with the words, 'It is not enough. We want more tanks, more planes, quicker arrivals, quicker discharge.'

Brundle's arrival – unfreezing of the ship and discharging of the cargo

There was no celebration party to mark PQ-8's arrival in Murmansk on 20 January 1942. As soon as *Harmatris* berthed, work was started to free the steam pipes of ice, a three-day job before the cargo was started on. This was not finished until the next month, all the cargo being discharged by 4 February.

More than seven-eighths of the cargo was sound and intact. Most of the damaged cargo was in No. 1 hold. Of fifteen lorries carried, two were useless, and 750 tons of sugar were lost. Temperatures sank to 40 degrees below zero. On 5 February *Harmatris* was ordered to berth at No. 6 quay to wait for dry dock.

The ship listed heavily to starboard. Very little steam had been raised during the discharge of the cargo due to the frozen state of the steam pipes. Ice and snow piled up on the decks, and together with the ship's listing, led to an almost impossible situation. A small fire broke out among the stoke-hold ashes. The bulkhead of the cadets' room became red hot, which in turn, set fire to the wardrobe in the cadets' room, destroying their clothing. After a two-hour struggle with buckets of water and stirrup pumps, the fire was extinguished. The crew of *Harmatris* were by now well used to fighting fires.

A battered, damaged ship

Even with the starboard list *Harmatris* entered dry dock on 10 February. The ship was well down by the head. The draft was 21 feet forward, and 11 feet aft. Members of the British Military Mission came on board and inspected the damage with the captain.

There was a large hole in the starboard bow, 60 feet by 30 feet. No. 1 ballast tank was shattered, and the bulkheads were badly damaged. On the port side was an ugly bulge stretching from the upper deck to about 14 feet. Rivets were missing and extensive damage had been caused to decks and other parts of the vessel. Repairs to the engine-room were necessary, and yet it was proving difficult to obtain parts or help with labour.

The captain sent out relays of men to ask for spare parts, if they could be spared from other ships. Labour was almost non-existent, and this lack of workmen, not to mention the absence of necessary parts, together with the freezing-cold weather, brought the work to a standstill.

Add to this a further disappointment. On 11 March Brundle was informed that he would have to vacate the dock so that a British destroyer damaged below the waterline could be repaired, which had the effect of shattering news after the previous and recent trials of *Harmatris*.

Banished from dry dock to a coal wharf

The crew was angry. So was the captain, who voiced his and the crew's objections. But it was of no avail. Escort destroyers were needed more urgently than a repaired *Harmatris*, sailing in ballast back to the UK. In the end objections by captain and crew were overruled by Admiral Bevan, the Senior British Naval Officer in North Russia. *Harmatris* vacated the dock on 14 March, and berthed at a coal wharf 4 miles from Murmansk, quite close to Vaenga, where, in the words of the captain, they were 'eventually forgotten'.

There now began a bleak period of utter neglect of *Harmatris*. No assistance was offered by the Russians. Engineers in the crew of *Harmatris* volunteered to carry on with repairs if overtime was paid. Brundle consulted Lieutenant Commander Miller of the Sea Transport Organisation (STO) and this was agreed. Even in these extreme conditions, the crew of *Harmatris* functioned in an organisation in which wages and overtime were part of the crew's *raison d'être*. Also, for a good crew, like the one that manned *Harmatris*, reward sweetened toil, and a great deal of toil and effort was needed to sort out the needs of the engine-room.

The need for an electric pump

Meanwhile, water was rising in No. 2 hold all of the time. An absolute need, to prevent the water building up and causing a dangerous listing for *Harmatris*, was a workable electric pump. Brundle spent hours going through all the British/Soviet liaison agencies on the telephone. He was narrowly dissuaded from sending a telegram to Stalin. A cable to the owners explained his despair and desperation, and he was promised by them that something would be done. And meanwhile, the only labour to hand was that provided by girls aged between 16 and 18.

Brundle's engineers, despite the almost total absence of Russian assistance, got on with the repairs and made some headway. Much of the work done earlier by Russian workmen had to be done again.

A small step forward was the return of *Harmatris* to the dry dock on 6 June, three months from the time they had to vacate it. All repairs carried out now and subsequently were those made by the crew of *Harmatris*. What prevented repair work, now that Brundle and the crew were back in Murmansk, was the constant bombing.

During the almost incessant air raids on the docks of Murmansk, the crew of *Harmatris*, with their DEMS gunners, stood to their weapons throughout entire air raids. The difficulty was that the enemy aircraft flew in very low to bomb and strafe, so that the AA gunners could not depress the barrels of their guns to get a sufficiently accurate targeting.

There was a particularly vicious raid on 24 March by 100 German planes, and a devastating attack in June. Eleven were shot down from the March raid. On 3 April, a veteran of PQ-13, and of the very first convoy, 'Dervish', to sail to Russia in August 1941, *New Westminster City* had been gravely damaged by four bombs, while another PQ-13 ship, *Empire Starlight*, seemed to be subjected to every kind of punishment, culminating in a dramatic sinking in dock on 16 June.

HMS *Gossamer*, one of the minesweeping flotilla at the edge of the Kola inlet, and which had assisted *Harmatris*, was sunk by Stukas on 24 June.

Ships sunk at their berths in Murmansk

New Westminster City, whose Master was Captain Harris, belonged to Reardon Smith of Cardiff. She was a veteran of PQ-13, and on the night of 3 April 1942 she was hit by four bombs from a Ju 88 during one of the air raids. The First Officer, Galer, leapt aboard *New Westminster City* during the air raid with other members of the crew to fight the fire.

One of the bombs exploded in No. 2 hold, in which was stored, among other things, a vast quantity of ammunition. One of the gunners, manning the starboard-bridge Oerlikon, was blown out of his gunpit and onto the quay. Amazingly, he suffered nothing more than light bruises, and returned to his post. Ammunition in No. 2 hold was now exploding and sending crackling and pinging sounds all round. The men took cover occasionally, but, for the main part, fought the fire with total disregard for personal safety.

Next door to *New Westminster City*, at the very next berth in Murmansk, *Empire Starlight* was also fighting a battle to put out flames, sustained in a hit by a stick of bombs.

Her bridge and midships accommodation were gutted by fire, and the only intact area of living accommodation was that occupied by DEMS gunners under the poop.

All fires aboard *Empire Starlight* were eventually put out. Her Chief Officer, J. Booth, doubled on the ship as Gunnery Officer. He was specially commended by the Master, Captain Stein. Meanwhile, the ship was moved to a less busy area of the docks, where the battle to keep her afloat and to prevent her becoming the victim of a dangerous listing continued. Cargo was discharged in the intervals between firefighting, defending the ship during air raids, and pumping the water out of the bilges. The excellent gunnery team shot down one Ju 88. On 16 June the gallant *Empire Starlight*, after settling by the head, was sunk. Only one member of the crew, a Chinese steward, was killed, ashore in an air raid.

Earlier, on 14 April, another ship berthed in Murmansk, another survivor, from convoy PQ-12, was sunk during an air raid after putting up the stoutest defence. One bomb penetrated three of her holds, Nos. 1, 2 and 3, and blew up with such force that the bottom of the ship was blown out. All her gallant crew managed to abandon ship in good order. Eleven Russian dock workers were killed.

Brundle's verdict, on witnessing all this heroism and tragedy, was expressed as follows. Remember that these things were witnessed in the heat of several air raids, while his DEMS gunners blazed away at incoming bombers.

> The SS Lancaster Castle *was eventually sunk at her anchorage by bombing, and the SS* New Westminster City *is burned out, and the SS* Empire Starlight *is deliberately thrown away through lack of co-operation by the Russians. This latter ship could have been repaired in a short time, and could have sailed home safely. She was only slightly damaged in one of the raids, but was ordered later to go to an anchorage near the SS* Lancaster Castle, *and was eventually sunk by bombs.*

Captain Stein, the Master, and Mr Morgan, the Chief Engineer of *Empire Starlight*, were awarded OBEs.

Many of PQ-13's recently arrived ships were becoming casualties in Murmansk. After defending herself vigorously against aircraft while coming into the Kola inlet, the Free Polish vessel SS *Tobruk* succumbed to a Murmansk air raid. An American freighter, *Deer Lodge*, was another casualty, after a stormy convoy, PQ-15, when it seemed every ship had to fight its way through, nautical mile by nautical mile. *Alcoa Cadet*, another American ship from PQ-15, was mysteriously sunk by an internal explosion, while in Murmansk dock, a third American ship, *Steel Worker*, struck a mine and sank, the victim, no doubt, of a mine sown in the Murmansk roads. SS *Ocean Voice*, Commodore's ship in PQ-16, and the Russian *Starii Bolshevik* both arrived in dock from that convoy with a horrific amount of bomb damage, with parts of the ships almost blasted away. Brundle wrote of how moved he was to see the damage to *Starii Bolshevik*, which had set out with him in PQ-8 five months ago. He was moved no less when *Ocean Voice* was one of those sunk in the return convoy he participated in, QP-14.

To work at night, and sleep by day

Such sights, such experiences, with the nerves of crew and all personnel stretched taut, made Robert Brundle agree readily with the request of a deputation from the officers and crew of *Harmatris* to work at night and sleep by day. It was a most melancholy of outcomes to see a ship which had fought weather, U-boats, Heinkels and Junkers to reach Murmansk, only to be blown up at an overcrowded and chaotic wharf in the docks of Murmansk, during one of those apparently ceaseless enemy air attacks. Some of these ships had not had the time to discharge their cargo. It was still a tonnage war, these Arctic convoys, though of a fundamentally different kind from that being fought in the Atlantic. Churchill made speeches constantly justifying the Russian convoys. 'The operation is justified if only half gets through', he said. To Brundle the waste of a cargo of vital tonnage, bought with the lives of allied seamen – 'the bravest men afloat', Churchill called them, alluding to PQ-17 – and blown up after recent arrival in Murmansk, must emphatically be avoided, and he made provision for this not to happen in the case of his own ship, the SS *Harmatris*. The ship was therefore vacated from 7.00am to 9.00pm. A watchman, chosen in rotation from volunteers, was appointed, and remained on the ship during the daylight hours. Added to this was the presence of two Russian naval sentries on the ship's gangway day and night.

During the Murmansk period of the story of *Harmatris* in North Russia the dock was attacked thirty times. As a result of these explosions the ship shuddered and vibrated, shrapnel rained down upon the decks, and blast from the bombing caused minor damage.

Murmansk was literally five minutes' flying time from hostile enemy airfields, Finnish and Norwegian. It had already been badly bombed at the time of the first convoys. Most of the ordinary residents had been evacuated, but there was still a reduced population of essential workers and families.

Acute shortages of food

British merchant sailors in Murmansk and RN personnel from the escorts went very short of food during the heavy bombing of 1942, as did the civil population. The ration for children was 200 grams (7oz) of bread a day, as compared with 300 grams for the adults. In December 1943 the bread ration had shrunk to 75 grams. All this does not take account of the berries people ate from hedgerows; bark, for example, from birch trees, needles from pine trees, and grass and nettles when the snow melted and things began to grow. At the midpoint of his time in Murmansk Robert Brundle recounted that he and the crew got a little fish occasionally, but mostly ate black bread on short rations. In desperation members of the crew of *Harmatris* rowed a small boat for 4 miles out into the Kola inlet and, with the consent of the STO, were able to get some tinned foodstuffs from partially sunken ships. Had Brundle been unable to obtain some foods from another J. & C. Harrison ship that arrived with a recent convoy, the situation would have been parlous in the extreme for the crew of *Harmatris*. The same daily drama and constant search for food was repeated time and again among the crews of other merchant ships stranded in Murmansk and Archangel.

Brundle's reports give a telling picture of being forgotten

At this time, the nadir of the fortunes of *Harmatris*, I quote from the report of Captain Brundle to the Admiralty. He writes both about the ship, and the food shortages, about searching for a pump to cure the excessive listing of the ship by pumping out the bilges, and about the perpetual hunger and shortages of food and the daily agonies of this. I reproduce some of the report, as follows, in full, although some of the issues have been already touched on, so that you may be able to recapture something of the desperation, desperation on the cusp of despair, endured by the Master and crew of *Harmatris*, and their search for a solution to these and other intractable problems.

> *The ship assumed a most uncomfortable position, and water was gaining in No. 2 hold all the time. After persistent phone calls and threatening to report the matter to Moscow, we eventually got an electric pump placed on board, and we were then able to keep the ship in a somewhat decent trim. Owing to the extreme cold, the work done in the drydock on the pipes etc. was undone through lack of attention and assistance from the shore.*
>
> *The question of fresh provisions now arises. We are unable to obtain any from the shore, and we have to await the arrival of a convoy, in which one of our ships is expected to arrive, and I am lucky enough to obtain a quantity of foodstuffs from them. The question of transport is also a difficult one. No one seems to want to assist us at all, and this inattention is beginning to show itself among the crew. I have already had several complaints from them about the food and the length of stay in port due to lack of cooperation and organisation.*
>
> *Another trouble has arisen. Air raids are now becoming frequent, and we are manning the guns several times a day.*
>
> *Severe snow storms and gales are now frequent, and the ship is covered to a depth of three feet. Everyone is working under difficulties. Foodstuffs are very scarce, and yeast unobtainable. We get a little fish occasionally, and are now eating black bread. We are having to go on short rations, and*

discontent is spreading among the crew. They want to be sent home and so to be able to join another ship or ships, and do something useful, instead of having to stay on board here, being subjected to bombing day by day.

HMS casualties are now arriving and we are still unable to get back into the drydock until these ships have been repaired. Air raids are becoming more numerous and great damage is being done to the town and ships in harbour. Convoys arriving now show a greater number of ships being lost, and several of those arriving are suffering from bomb damage.

I have been promised that we shall go into dock on May 8, but, when that day arrived, it was postponed to the 16th, and then to the 31st. I am fed up, and send a cable to my Owners to see if anything can be done from the English side, as I am sure that we are being entirely ignored here.

I wonder if my cable home has had any effect, because I am now informed that, if my ship is not re-docked on June 1, the British government are going to take action. We did not dock on the 1st, and on the 3rd the SS Yaka *went into dock for forty-eight hours. Another convoy arrives, and among the arrivals is the SS* Ocean Voice *and the Russian SS* Starii Bolshevik, *both damaged by bombs.*

If we do not get into dock before these ships are discharged, we shall be again disappointed. Their repairs can be done afloat, but they may have to dock for further examination.

Some of our super heat elements came back from the repair shop, and, on examination my Chief Engineer states that they have not been touched. He found holes in some of them. A lot of the work that has been done by the Russians has had to be done over again by my engineers. My windlass is still unusable, and no work has been done on it, since we arrived. Owing to constant air raids, work is now being suspended by day and resumed at night. There is a great shortage of skilled men and men labour. Young girls of 16 and 18 are employed on the welding and other repair work.

We eventually re-docked at midnight on June 6 1942. Work on repairs proceeds at a faster pace, and we can now see signs of getting home.

Fraternisation

Fraternisation with Russian girls in the North Russian ports was near to impossible (relations with any kind of Russian personnel were strictly forbidden), although, inevitably, some sailors, both of the merchant service and RN, were good at avoiding and dodging the multiple pitfalls and restrictions. And yet carnal temptations withered in the bitter cold, while harsh punishments for fraternisation (up to ten years in a labour camp for some poor girls) did the rest.

An attempt to loosen up relations between Russian civilians and allied personnel was made in 1943 when a hall was opened in Murmansk, called *Dom Druzhby, imeni Vinstona Churchkhilya*, 'The Winston Churchill House of Friendship'. There was food (meagre and severely restricted, of course), music and dancing. Inevitably some relationships began to flourish, in contrast to the repressive regime of 1941 and 1942; but for all the Intourist Hotels and International Clubs beginning to develop in the ports, it was still a risky thing for a Russian girl to make a date with an allied seaman.

Russian interpreters

At the officers' club in Polyarnoe meetings of officers of RN escorts with their counterparts in the Red Navy did take place. The club was restricted to officers of both services, but, inevitably, tended to remain a Royal Navy preserve.

One officer of a British escort ship recalls an evening at this club in Polyarnoe when he tasted caviar for the first time, an astonishing anomaly in view of the food shortages already chronicled, and noteworthy because of its utter rarity. The same officer recalls on this memorable evening being shown a long reel of the famous Russian film by Eisenstein (doyen of today's Arts Cinemas) *Ivan the Terrible*. A modicum of mutual understanding was arrived at because of naval personnel of proven linguistic ability being trained as Russian interpreters. A number of these, who were put through a crash course at Cambridge, were taught by the celebrated Cambridge Russianist, Dr Elizabeth Hill, whose achievements in her legendary Russian classes bordered on the miraculous. Her pupils became fluent Russian interpreters in the North Russian ports, staying for months at a time until they were relieved. Their expertise, astonishing fluency in the language, despite the artificiality and haste of the Russian course's inception, and their readiness to go anywhere they were needed, from the highest echelons of naval councils to a low-level but potentially damaging dispute between sailors of the two nationalities, did amazing things for Soviet–allied understanding in such difficult and apparently unpromising conditions.

There was a tendency, whenever the seasons and the absence of ice blocking up the mouth of the Dvina River permitted it, to get allied ships out of the Kola inlet and away from Murmansk to Archangel (Archangelsk in Russian), to relieve the over-crowding and as a refuge from the bombing. Brundle now, in July 1942, received a signal from the Senior British Naval Officer, North Russia, Rear Admiral R.H. Bevan, to proceed to Archangel, and preparations were made accordingly.

Brundle's report, in the process of preparing to leave Murmansk, commits to paper some sober reflections on the shortages of food in all the Russian ports.

> When we left Murmansk I learned that the town had practically been wiped out, and casualties were very high indeed. At Archangel we found it very difficult to be supplied with foodstuffs. My ship was not the only one to have suffered. All the captains were constantly on the prowl for food, and had to return to the ship without any hope. When some of the captains approached the Russian authorities about food, they were told that food would be supplied when Britain started a second front.

'Second Front' now

This insistence that the allies should embark on a 'Second Front' right now was a hoary old chestnut, a *canard* used to chastise the allies and kick-start their jammed strategies, from the mouths of Russian commissars (as seen here) in the Arctic ports and of British 'Second Front Now' enthusiasts in the streets of London, of Franklin Delano Roosevelt and of Joseph Stalin. It was embodied in the first request made by Stalin to Churchill immediately after the German invasion of Russia: couldn't Britain embark on a Second Front in France in 1942 to divert and draw off the German troops from destroying the Soviet Union? The absurdity of such an all-out, high-risk commitment, without the proper preparation of winning other battles first, in other strategic theatres of war, was pushed aside, as more and more the notion of a Second Front acquired a mythical, almost a mystical significance.

Nevertheless it was a notion entertained by some serious politicians. It became a resignation issue early on in the war for Beaverbrook. When Churchill, in one of his private meetings with Stalin, had the unpalatable task of saying 1) that the Second Front could not be mounted until well into 1943 (it took, of course, a year longer than this) and 2) that the Russian convoys, after the failure of PQ-17, would have to be discontinued for a while, Stalin retorted, with a measure of anger, that you could not make war without losses, and that the Soviet Union was losing 10,000 fighting men a day.

PQ-17: ships and men

Just before leaving the Kola inlet on 21 July 1942 Brundle got to know about the decimation of convoy PQ-17, and that *Hartlebury* and *Empire Byron* were among the ships sunk.

This event is significant, as PQ-17 ships and survivors sailed back with Brundle in QP-14. When PQ-17 sailed from Hvalfiordur on 27 June 1942 the weather was fine and it was noted that the icecap had receded further than usual at this particular season. Convoy PQ-17 was made up of 36 merchant ships, most of them American (a sign of the times). The long litany of names of the 36 ships is worth reciting here, as we shall encounter and refer to several of them, both in PQ-17's tragic story, in particular, and in the account of the return convoy, QP-14, in which Brundle and *Harmatris* sailed.

Brundle was to meet many of the ships of PQ-17 and the survivors among their crews (some of whom sailed aboard *Harmatris* in convoy QP-14) in the months ahead.

From port to starboard, therefore, the convoy emerged, as they sailed on that fine July morning, as follows:

First: *Paulus Potter* (Dutch), *Washington* (American), *Hartlebury* (British and Vice commodore). This last was a J. & C. Harrison ship, like *Harmatris* (remember the 'Ha' – signature letters at the beginning of each ship), and her Master, Captain Stephenson, was a friend of Brundle. Sadly he was to receive a head wound diving from his ship in her last moments before sinking, from which he died. Brundle saw him in Archangel and visited him before he left in QP-14.

Continuing the roll there was *Pan Atlantic* (American), *River Afton* the Commodore ship, which was British. Commodore of PQ-17 and in this ship was John Dowding RNR, who was to have his ship sunk from under him in this convoy and in QP-14. He had been twenty years in the Orient Line in the Merchant Navy, after a period of RN service in the First World War, and he had come back into the Royal Navy for the duration of this war.

There were then *Empire Byron* (with her Master, Captain Wharton, also well known to Brundle and later visited by him in Archangel), which was British, *Christopher Newport* (whose crew behaved near mutinously in the course of this voyage) and *Samuel Chase*, both brand-new American Liberty ships.

The second rank were *Hoosier* (American), *El Capitan* (Panamanian), *Pankraft* (American), *Navarino* (British) and *Azerbaijan* (Russian, running with, to everyone's astonishment, a largely female crew). Then *Earlston* (British), *Benjamin Harrison* (another brand-new American Liberty ship), *Fairfield City* and *Carlton* (both American).

The third rank, from port to starboard again, sailed as *Ironclad* (American), *Bolton Castle* (British), *Olopana*, *Bellingham* and *Alcoa Ranger* (all American), then the British CAM ship *Empire Tide*, the British freighter *Ocean Freedom* and the American *Honomu*, and *Daniel Morgan*.

In the fourth rank sailed *William Hooper* (American), *Troubadour* (Panamanian), *Donbass* (Russian), *Silver Sword* and *Winston Salem* (both American), the British fleet oiler *Aldersdale*, and another American Liberty ship, *John Witherspoon*. Bringing up the rear were the three British rescue ships *Rathlin*, *Zaafaran* and *Zamalek*.

The names of these ships will reappear later. Twenty-four of them would not reach the North Russian ports, but would end up at the bottom of the Barents Sea.

There was an initial light escort from Iceland, three minesweepers and four trawlers when the convoy sailed from Hvalfiordur. On 30 June Commander J.E. Broome, the Senior Escort Officer, arrived in the destroyer *Keppel*, one of eight destroyers and three corvettes. Two AA ships, *Pozarica* and *Palomares*, converted from fruit carriers, sailed between the second and third ranks, and there were two submarines.

There was also the heavy cruiser support of Rear Admiral 'Turtle' Hamilton's four cruisers led by his own flagship, HMS *London*. They were *Norfolk*, and the American ships, USS *Tuscaloosa* and *Wichita*, with one British and two American destroyers. Their brief was to see that PQ-17 got to the USSR, but also, in a free-ranging capacity, to draw out heavy German surface vessels, and, if possible, decoy them and lead their attention away from the Home Fleet.

The convoy passed in and out of fog banks, and there were a number of U-boat scares. The cruiser heavy support sailed with Admiral Hamilton 40 miles to the north. Poor weather over Norway prevented effective reconnaissance, even though a Walrus was up from HMS *London*, and a Blohm und Voss BV 138 was shadowing the convoy.

Movements of German heavy ships were occurring, and contributed to the subsequent confusion. *Lützow*, *Scheer*, and six German destroyers had left their base at Narvik, but, because of the atrocious fog, encountered difficulty. *Lützow* ran aground and some destroyers hit uncharted rocks.

Misleading intelligence sources

It was at this point that intelligence sources, emanating from Sweden, came to the Admiralty about German intentions. These affirmed and pointed to an attack on the convoy between longitudes 15 and 30 east. The Admiralty received this intelligence early on 4 July, when the convoy had sailed to a position almost exactly midway between the two points.

It must be said that it did seem, both from the testimony of the intelligence reports and the movement of the German surface ships, as if an attack upon the convoy by a combined heavy force could be expected.

PQ-17 is attacked

Sixty miles north of Bear Island the convoy was attacked by an He 111. The Heinkel's torpedo missed the AA ship *Palomares* but continued on its track and struck *Christopher Newport*, the American Liberty ship, which had 10,000 tons of munitions aboard. *Zamalek* was soon alongside, taking off forty-seven survivors. Commander Broome, the jaunty Senior Escort Officer who inspired the merchantmen with such confidence at one of the pre-convoy conferences, ordered one of the submarines, *P-614*, to torpedo *Christopher Newport*. This was indeed, attempted; but the job of sinking the troubled vessel had to be left to a real enemy, *U-457*, on a later occasion.

Hamilton, meanwhile, took his cruiser force to a position 12 miles ahead of the convoy, ordering Broome, in *Keppel*, to change course to the north-east. The Luftwaffe, who, of course, had the convoy under observation, were misled into believing that an anti-submarine aircraft flown off USS *Wichita* had come from an aircraft carrier. This misconception, coupled with the fact that they also believed that the Home Fleet was much nearer than it in fact was (when it was, in actuality, 350 miles away from the convoy), meant that the German surface force, with all their lethal armaments, could not, would not, sail, because Hitler had insisted absolutely that any aircraft carrier had to be put out of action first.

The U-boats, amply alerted by their shadowing BV 138, homed in on the convoy, firing their torpedoes. Coupled with this, twenty-five He 111s of KG 26 and several Ju 88s of KG 30, carrying torpedoes, attacked the convoy from astern. The merchantman *Navarino* was struck. A blazing Heinkel He 111 hit the sea, and seamen on the ships of the convoy could see burning airmen – the sea war was cruel – as she sank. Leutnant Hennemann had flown an astonishingly brave sortie. He was awarded the Knight's Cross posthumously.

The Liberty ship *William Hooper* sustained a torpedo hit from one of the Heinkels that followed Hennemann, and her boiler exploded. Cruisers from Hamilton's force continued their firepower. The Soviet tanker *Azerbaijan* exploded after another torpedo hit. Nevertheless she survived, because she was carrying linseed oil, which does not possess the same destructive power as fuel oil. *Zamalek* rescued a boatload of survivors, which the Master of the tanker refused to have back on board, as they were deserters. Such was nihilistic Russian logic!

Signals from the Admiralty

At 21.11 hours on 3 July the Admiralty signalled both Hamilton and Tovey: 'CRUISER FORCE TO WITHDRAW TO WESTWARD AT HIGH SPEED.'

Because of all those warnings about the fast closing of enemy surface units, there was a clear impression, which grew, as time passed, into a conviction that *Tirpitz* was at sea. Recalling PQ-17's tragedy and remembering the faltering steps, the unravelling of the signals and the deepening and hardening of the detailed background impressions that led up to this, Admiral Sir Dudley Pound's Second-in-Command, Sir Henry Moore (Vice-Chief of the Naval Staff) said:

> *All the discussion was on the basis that* Tirpitz *was at sea. I was completely convinced of it. Perhaps some chance remark had planted it in the back of our minds.*

> *Daily Mail*, 18 February 1970

Admiral Pound, at this juncture, disregarded Paymaster Commander Denning's assurance that no indication that *Tirpitz* was at sea had been received from either agents' reports or Enigma decrypts from Bletchley Park. We must remember, however, that Pound and Denning had received information from Swedish intelligence sources, forwarded by Captain Henry Denham (not to be confused with Denning, above), even before the convoy of merchantmen had sailed from Hvalfiordur, of the German master plan, with the Wagnerian appellation of

Rösselsprung, 'The Knight's Move'. Part of this master plan, after initial air reconnaissance, and so on, was to order bombing attacks on the convoy from the North Norwegian airfields when PQ-17 reached Jan Mayen Island. Then it was that ... 'Pocket battleships and six destroyers will move to Altenfiord ... *Tirpitz* and *Hipper* to Narvik. Naval forces may be expected to operate ... once convoy has receded five degrees east.'

You would think that the presence on or absence from the sea lanes of the dreaded *Tirpitz* could be irrefutably established by prompt air reconnaissance. An accident to a Catalina flying boat had ruled out any such prompt and ready validation of this crucial situation, so one could not be sure. On the other hand a cluster of chattering signals indicated a powerful U-boat presence.

'Convoy is to scatter'

The Admiralty believed in themselves as sole arbiters and masters of the situation in crises of this type, in full possession of all the facts. Pound, the First Sea Lord, thought it unfair to place any absolute executive responsibility in such a scenario on the shoulders of Commander Broome, once 'Turtle' Hamilton and his cruisers had left, so Pound advocated dispersing the convoy. Moore advised this would take too long. The quicker this dispersal was to be effected, the safer and better it would all be. And so the infamous and fate-laden and terrible signal came to be sent: 'CONVOY IS TO SCATTER.'

What to do? There was a kind of cordon or corridor between where the Arctic icecap ended and the coast of Norway. Through this the ships must pass to reach Russia. These last stages in this ever-narrowing corridor were the most dangerous for the merchantmen. For this was where the U-boats attacked, with the proximity of the Kola inlet and Kildin Island creating hiding places for predatory submarines. This was also where the He 111s and Ju 88s took off from Norwegian airfields to torpedo and bomb vessels. This was, after all, where a surface fleet might corner them, and blow them out of the water.

The signal meant that Hamilton must sail to the west, and that Broome, as Senior Escort Officer, must be on station to supervise the scattering. Dowding, in *River Afton*, at the head of the centre column, just did not understand. Broome had to bring *Keppel* up close and repeat the signal through a megaphone. He then expended his infinite regret in inimitable naval signalese: 'sorry to leave you like this' was Broome's departing signal. 'Goodbye and good luck. It looks like a bloody business.'

Broome was choking with rage and shock. As indeed, all seamen, RN or merchantmen were, when they saw what was happening. Escort destroyers were given instructions to proceed to the Russian ports, while the ranks and columns of merchant ships peeled off and dissolved. The entire convoy dissolved, ceased to exist as a convoy, in bizarre fashion, with the centre column remaining in position while the other ships to port and starboard simply edged away, gathering speed when they were clear.

The Germans have a field day

Then it was time and opportunity for the Germans to rampage like hungry wolves among a flock of sheep. It was their *glückliche Zeit* (happy time). Early on 5 July, *U-334* made an attempt to torpedo *Navarino* (she sank before the torpedo arrived). But *U-334* got *William Hooper*. In the frantic alerting of Luftwaffe aircraft from Norway side by side with those ever-hungry U-boats, a Soviet submarine, *K-21*, spotted *Tirpitz*, and other ships with her, leaving Norway. The Russian fired his torpedoes and, alas, wasted chance – there were no hits.

This attack caused Grossadmiral Raeder to express caution to the captain of *Tirpitz*, and, by the time that the big German ships had been spotted by a Catalina, as well as by the British submarine *Unshaken*, the Germans, at the express order of Hitler himself (always hyper-cautious in such matters), recalled their capital ships to port to the extreme frustration and stunned disappointment of their captains. Here were *Tirpitz* and Germany's best ships, primed and ready. To cancel *Rösselsprung* was tantamount to cancelling Jutland (or the battle), to abolishing *Der Tag*. Sadly, soberly, and with infinite regret Kapitän Wagner, Chief of Naval Operations, summed up the situation: 'Every operation by our surface forces has been hampered by the Führer's desire to avoid losses and reverses at all costs.'

Hitler had a 'thing' about the Royal Navy, and he had a 'thing' about Norway as a sector the British were going to invade and control.

Nevertheless the Germans certainly made the best of the circumscribed situation and achieved abundantly the partial success Raeder desired.

British ships reacted to the ghastly signals and their consequences in different ways. *Pozarica* joined three corvettes and headed east with them. Four American merchant ships gathered round *Palomares* on 5 July, only to be discovered at 13.00 hours by a BV 138 flying boat. The naval vessels simply left them and steered for the Matochkin Strait, the stretch of water dividing the two islands of Novaya Zemlya, which in its turn divided the Barents Sea from the Kara Sea. The most northerly part of Novaya Zemlya was 5 degrees further north than Murmansk and the Kola inlet, part of the geography of the fabled North-East Passage.

This was an example of what has been called protective grouping, huddling together for security. In fact thirty-one allied merchant ships in all tried to make for and enjoy whatever protection Novaya Zemlya afforded. Eventually, however, they had to make for the Russian ports, on which errand, between 5 and 10 July, twenty of them were lost. In fact twenty-four ships, two-thirds of the convoy in all, were sunk.

Some of the last ships to arrive from the depleted convoy were *Azerbaijan, Silver Sword, Benjamin Harrison, Ironclad* and *Troubadour*. *Azerbaijan* was Russian, *Troubadour* was Panamanian, and the rest were American. Finally *Winston Salem*, another American ship, sailed into Archangel, as the only outstanding ship. She had had to have fuel oil pumped out of her to assist her rescue from ice.

In the middle of this holocaust some ships that have figured in our narrative so far became victims. The rescue ship *Zaafaran* was originally a German ship, seized by the British when war broke out, from the Pharaonic Mail Line. Both she and *Zamalek*, before they were commandeered and kitted out as rescue ships, operated trips across the channel and day trips on the Thames. *Zamalek* strove hard to rescue crew from *Zaafaran* when she was about to sink, the victim of a Ju 88. Battered, and loaded up to the Plimsoll line with survivors, the *Zamalek* reached Archangel on 11 July. She had stood by *Harmatris* in her hour of need in PQ-8.

The record of the rescue ships *Zaafaran*, *Zamalek* and little *Rathlin*, coming from diverse backgrounds to a sublime destiny on the cold Arctic seas, saving countless numbers of lives, was indeed a proud one.

Empire Byron and *Hartlebury* are sunk

One ship Brundle was familiar with was *Empire Byron*, a MOWT ship, which was managed by J. & C. Harrison. He knew the Master, Captain Wharton, the Vice Commodore of PQ-17. She was sunk, one of a number in the dreadful slaughter wreaked by U-boats, Ju 88s and He 111s on 5 July by *U-703*. A number of torpedoes slammed into her, sending her cargo of military vehicles high in the air, or over the side, or slamming into one another.

Captain Wharton told his officers to slash off their epaulettes from their greatcoats. U-boat crews were keen to take masters prisoner, or, failing that, to take any officer present back in their U-boat for interrogation and eventually to the Merchant Navy prisoner-of-war camp at Marlag and Milag Nord, not far from Bremen. When *U-703* surfaced alongside them in the lifeboat (as it did later for *Hartlebury* and for several other of their victims), Captain Wharton was not betrayed. However, a prisoner was taken; an army officer who was a passenger on *Empire Byron* to North Russia, so that he could act as an instructor to teach the members of the Red Army how to handle the new Churchill tanks that were being transported to Russia now.

The men in the boats were given some schnapps and a bit of food and *U-703* dived and left them. Eventually Wharton and his men were rescued, leaving eighteen dead shipmates in the ship as it went down.

Hartlebury, from the same ship-owners, and the Master of which, Captain Stephenson, was another of Brundle's friends, was sunk on 7 July by *U-355* when steaming to Novaya Zemlya's south island. Stephenson dived from the stern of the ship, maintaining the immortal tradition of the captain being the last man to leave. Beside a lifeboat *U-355* surfaced and demanded to have the ship's Master to take into custody. No one gave Stephenson away and he had taken off his jacket before the dive.

Eventually *Hartlebury*'s survivors received sanctuary on *Winston Salem*, which had run aground in the ice on Novaya Zemlya.

Among the catalogue of tragedy attending any sinking ship, individuals trapped below, those who died one by one in a lifeboat, and so on, there are two pieces of tragedy of particular poignancy bound up with the final end of *Hartlebury*.

One concerns her Master, Captain Stephenson, who dived from the stern of the ship, as he thought he was the last man to leave *Hartlebury*. Stephenson subsequently died from a head injury sustained in this dive from the stern. He was the only Master to be lost from PQ-17, although he died a while after the incident, as Brundle visited him and Captain Wharton in Archangel before his departure in QP-14.

The other item of poignant significance was that Captain Stephenson was not in fact the last man off *Hartlebury*, although he did not know this at the time. There was, in fact, another man on board, who had been left hanging in mid-air when the lifeboat he sought refuge in had been cut adrift. It was all up with him when another torpedo slammed into the vessel. He was now cut off from all hope and means of escape. He stood there waving at the lifeboat as it passed by, too far out by now to accomplish any future rescue, and needing to keep some distance from the sinking *Hartlebury*, lest the lifeboat should be dragged down along with the doomed vessel.

Men in the lifeboat saw him – it was Second Officer Harold Spence – waving to them from the bridge, taking off his life jacket, his coat, and even his cap. He knew it would not be long for him in the cold Arctic sea, and he had resolved to make a quick end of things. Harold Spence had been married ten days before *Hartlebury* had sailed from Sunderland on her final voyage. These are the tears of things, poignant tragedies in the wider picture of war and desolation.

Death toll of PQ-17 and aftermath

Twenty-four ships were sunk and 153 merchant seamen died in PQ-17. No Royal Navy personnel were killed. The Americans were particularly critical of the decision to scatter the convoy, with good reason, as they lost many ships and men.

As for the material and military equipment that had gone down with the twenty-four ships, this amounted to a total complement of 210 bombers, 430 tanks, 3,350 military vehicles and approximately 100,000 tons of ammunition.

Convoys to Russia were suspended. There were to be no more convoys until the return of the sheltering winter darkness. The Russian Ambassador in London, Ivan Maisky, became angry, and even more incensed when Admiral Sir Dudley Pound further agitated the Russians by saying that nothing could be done until better and more extended air cover could be provided from the Russian end.

As regards the decisions made for PQ-17 and the decision to scatter the convoy, it is a fact that *Tirpitz* and the other German surface vessels did not leave Altenfiord until the morning of 5 July, *after* the order scattering the convoy. And then, as we have demonstrated, the Germans, on the orders of Raeder, acting on Hitler's misgivings, abandoned the sortie of *Tirpitz* and the others that very same day.

QP-13, a homeward-bound convoy, also had bad luck at this time. Setting off a day earlier than PQ-17's departure from Hvalfiordur, 26 June 1942, with thirty-five merchant ships, mainly American and with some new Liberty ships, a frequent sight and presence in convoys from now onwards, all went well until 5 July. While coming through the Denmark Strait towards Iceland, they ran into a British minefield. An escorting minesweeper, HMS *Niger*, blew up, with many lives lost. Five merchant ships were sunk, and one was badly damaged by the mines.

QP-13's fate tends to be overlooked by historians in view of the overwhelming tragedy of PQ-17, which happened at the same time. That was the costliest convoy of all. Churchill himself called it 'one of the most melancholy episodes in the whole of the war'.

Brundle sails to Archangel

Brundle and *Harmatris* sailed from the Kola inlet on 21 July. The journey took them along the Murman coast, and round Cape Orlov into a narrow strait in the White Sea called Gourlo. It was this narrow piece of waterway that got blocked up with ice during the winter months. So harsh were the weather conditions that sometimes icebreakers were needed at other times of the year.

The approach to Archangel was by the Dvina River from the White Sea. Smaller ports lay to one side or another, Ekonomiya, a few miles north of Archangel, and Molotovsk, on the White Sea just before the Dvina River starts, with Bakaritsa, on the west bank of the Dvina.

The journey from the Kola inlet to Archangel was about 400 miles and took the best part of three days, 21 to 24 July. Out in the White Sea *Harmatris* would be in remote visual contact with the Solovetsky archipelago, islands out in the middle of the vast sea, monasteries originally, but, at the time *Harmatris* passed, the 'oldest gulag', or labour camp, in Russia, crammed full of political prisoners the Stalinist regime had condemned to hard labour. On 26 July *Harmatris* was sent up to Ekonomiya to discharge her ballast, and then to Myrmaxa to load 3,000 tons of steel pipes.

Like Murmansk, Archangel also seemed to have run out of food. Captains of the waiting merchant ships, like Brundle, of *Harmatris*, formed their own 'black market' underground network, so that, if and when there was any food to be had, their own ships and crews would get their fair share. Brundle also remarked in his report on the suspicious nature of most Russians, and the petty restrictions which surrounded them on their long stay in Murmansk and Archangel. One particular frustration, more intense than others, was that captains of ships could not visit each other on board their vessels, without a special pass from the NKVD (the Russian Secret Police), while the crew were forbidden to visit other ships at all. This was an especially tiresome restriction, seeing that no one objected to them meeting on the quay close to the ship, where they could and did socialise to their hearts' content.

A town of ragged survivors

The streets of Archangel were thronged with survivors of the PQ-17 tragedy. Brundle had visited the captains of *Hartlebury* and *Empire Byron* and he was to get to know a number of other survivors, who were to obtain passage on *Harmatris* in QP-14 and to travel with him and his crew. It was certainly a rather crowded trip for the return journey.

Up to this return journey Archangel was a bleak, aimless gathering point for those who had escaped the decimation of PQ-17 and other convoys, and for those who, like *Harmatris* and her crew, had been taken out of circulation by months of enforced waiting. There were precious few leisure facilities in any of the Russian ports, but there was in Archangel an Interclub, which, with survivors not properly kitted out, and clutching their own and recently acquired possessions several sizes too big for them, bore every resemblance to a rather untidy or badly organised Left-Luggage Office.

Of course, Archangel's main attraction, some would say its only attraction, was that it did not get attacked so often, and almost bombed out of existence, like Murmansk. There were not as many berths for ships as Murmansk had; but the absence of the bombing made up for that. The surrounding countryside, however, was monotonous, flat and featureless, which, for those blocked in by ice in the Gourlo Strait at a certain season in the year, increased the sense of abandonment they felt. It was easy to feel sidelined and forgotten when even the icebreakers, sent with you to force a passage, suffered the common fate of being frozen in with you.

Robert Brundle, however, was gradually becoming aware that the Murmansk/Archangel adventure would soon be over. He quietly made his preparations for return, and encouraged members of the crew of *Harmatris* to do likewise.

All the time in Archangel Brundle was waiting for news of a return convoy home for him and the crew of *Harmatris*. By September he and his crew were virtually 'under starter's orders', and on 13 September *Harmatris* sailed from the Dvina lightship in a convoy of twenty ships, QP-14.

Captain Robert Brundle, a
pre-war photograph.
(*Michael Wadsworth*)

Captain Robert Brundle
at the Investiture.
(*Hull Daily Mail*)

SS *Harmatris* in peacetime livery. *(Welsh Industrial Museum, Cardiff)*

SS *Harmatris* in wartime. (*Michael Wadsworth*)

SS *Harberton*, Brundle's post-war ship, involved in the 'Corfu Incident'. (*Michael Wadsworth*)

Captain Wharton, MBE, DSC, Master
of the *Empire Byron*, sunk on PQ17.
(*Michael Wadsworth*)

An ammunition ship 'goes up'
in one of the Russian convoys.
(*Catriona Macleod via Iain G Smith*)

An Arctic convoy is attacked. (*Catriona Macleod via Iain G Smith*)

Repairs carried out on SS *Harmatris* in dry dock in Murmansk. (*Michael Wadsworth*)

HMS *Eskimo* is attacked on convoy PQ18. HMS *Eskimo* in foreground, with *HMS Wheatland*'s stern just visible, clear of bomb blast. (*Catriona Macleod via Iain G Smith*)

HMS *Speedwell.*
(*Michael Wadsworth*)

HMS *Matabele.* (*Michael Wadsworth*)

SHIP FIRED — TORPEDOED — BOMBED — ABANDONED — REBOARDED — AND YET SHE REACHED RUSSIA

LE NAVIRE FUT INCENDIE, TORPILLE, BOMBARDE, ABANDONNE, PUIS REOCCUPE PAR L'EQUIPAGE, MAIS IL ARRIVA EN RUSSIE

This is what happened to their ship:

Voici l'histoire de leur bâtiment:

Captain Robert Brundle wins the O.B.E.
Le Capitaine Robert Brundle reçoit le O.B.E. (Officer of the Order of the British Empire).
Captein Robert Brundle vinner O.B.E.
Captain Robert Brundle ontvangt de O.B.E.

1 Fire breaks out but is extinguished.
Un incendie éclate, mais on l'éteint.
Det begynte à brenne men blev slukket.
Er brak brand uit, maar deze werd gebluscht.

Chief Officer Masterman wins the M.B.E.
Masterman, Premier Officier, reçoit le M.B.E. (Member of the Order of the British Empire).
Førstestyrmann Masterman vinner M.B.E.
Chief Officer Masterman ontvangt de M.B.E.

4 ...while he and other officers inspect the damage.
...pendant qu'il inspecte les dégâts avec les autres officiers.
...mens han og andre officerer besiktiger skaden.
...terwijl hij en de officieren de schade gingen opnemen.

Chief Steward Peart, awarded the B.E.M.
Peart, Maître d'Hôtel, reçoit le B.E.M. (British Empire Medal).
Restauratør Peart, vinner B.E.M.
Chief Steward Peart krijgt de B.E.M.

7 She is towed through air attacks and...
Le bâtiment est remorqué à travers les attaques aériennes ennemies...
Det slepes gjennem luftangrep og...
Het schip werd onder hevige luchtaanvallen verder gesleept

The story of SS *Harmatris* and of PQ8 from the *Neptune* Merchant Navy Magazine for July 1943. (*Michael Wadsworth*)

Dette er hvad som hendte deres skip:

Het volgende gebeurde met hun schip:

...er the ship is twice torpedoed.
...tard, le navire est torpillé à deux reprises.
...ere blev skipet torpedert to ganger.
...arna werd het tweemaal getorpedeerd.

3 The Captain orders the crew to the boats...
Le Capitaine commande à l'équipage de mettre les canots de sauvetage à la mer...
Kapteinen beordrer mannskapet til båtene...
De kapitein gaf het bevel de booten te strijken...

...hird explosion! They transfer to another ship.
...troisième explosion! Ils montent à bord d'un autre navire.
...tredje eksplosjon. De flytter over til ett annet skip.
...derde explosie volgde! Zij werden op een ander schip
...rgebracht.

6 Three hours pass—they decide to reboard.
Trois heures se passent. Ils décident de revenir à leur bord.
Efter tre timers forløp bestemmer de å borde igjen.
Na drie uur werd besloten weer aan boord te gaan.

...eaches Russia with a valuable cargo...
...t arrive en Russie avec sa précieuse cargaison...
...nkommer til Rusland med sin dyrebare last...
...n wist Rusland te bereiken met zijn kostbare lading...

9 ...of war equipment for the Soviet Army.
...de ravitaillements de guerre pour l'Armée des Soviets.
...bestående av utstyr til den russiske armè.
...oorlogsmateriaal voor het Soviet-leger.

HMS *Sharpshooter.* (*Michael Wadsworth*)

HMS *Harrier.* (*Michael Wadsworth*)

A pre-convoy conference of ships' Masters and radio officers. Notice the mixture of civilian dress ('owners rig'), with Merchant Navy uniform.
(*Imperial War Museum A4551*)

HMS *Avenger.* (*Imperial War Museum FL1268*)

Ice on HMS *Belfast* during a Russian convoy. (*Imperial War Museum 20687*)

HMS *Belfast* off Iceland. (*Imperial War Museum 15530*)

HMS *Scylla* – crew clearing away ice on an Arctic convoy. (*Imperial War Museum A15365*)

Explosion of the ammunition ship, the American *Mary Luckenbach* on convoy PQ18. (*Imperial War Museum A12225*)

Consolidated Catalina 1B (FP 115 'U'). Flown by F/S Semmens and crew. Sunk U253 115 miles north of Iceland during QP14 on 23 September 1942. (*via Andy Thomas*)

CAM ship *Empire Tide*. Survived PQ17 and came back on QP14, Brundle's return convoy. (*Imperial War Museum A9422*)

CHAPTER 7

A Costly Return: QP-14

And now there came both mist and snow
And it grew wondrous cold,
And ice, mast high, came floating by,
As green as emerald.

Samuel Taylor Coleridge, 'The Rime
of the Ancient Mariner' (1798)

Joy, warm as the joy that shipwrecked sailors feel,
When they catch sight of land.

Homer, *The Odyssey* 23:262 (8th century BC)

By September 1942 the waiting time for a home-bound convoy
was over, and *Harmatris* joined convoy QP-14, sailing from Archangel up the Dvina River on 13 September 1942, an auspicious or
inauspicious day, depending on how the sailors interpreted their
current superstitions. QP-14 was a large convoy, and *Harmatris*
was one of twenty merchant ships composing it.

A cold start

The day was not one of calm weather. It was cold, the wind
howled, drizzle stung faces, and though it was autumn, there
was the feeling that winter was not far away. There were a
number of surviving vessels from PQ-17, together with others,

119

like *Harmatris*, who had been waiting for months in the North Russian ports for a convoy home. The waiting and the longing for home was compounded by the fact that convoys were suspended after the utter disaster of PQ-17, despite Stalin's chagrin and rage, which Churchill got used to handling. Brundle had got used, particularly in Murmansk, to watching badly damaged ships limp to their berths, and, inadequately protected from the threat of bombing, get blown up, with some loss of life, a short time later. There were, therefore, inevitably, a large, an increasingly large number of survivors of ships of the convoy PQ-17 and of other doomed ships. They had given a special character to Archangel, which contained an enormous number of these dispossessed tatterdemalions, wandering the streets, most of them hungry, and some of them ill-clad. The convoy QP-14 was going to rescue and transport all these survivors. It would irrevocably change the streets of Archangel, empty them at a stroke. Archangel, where all these refugees had foregathered was, very largely, a city made of wood, and hundreds of troops and ordinary civilians and allied merchantmen turned out with buckets and hoses to tackle raging fires when enemy bombs came. They did not come as often to Archangel as they did to Murmansk, but they came, nevertheless. The merchantmen sought to protect the shipping in Archangel. So their hoses were on playing over their ships during the bombing raids.

Before QP-14 left, mail, food and coal came. To beguile remaining weeks of waiting one felicitous event was the arrival of the first mail for some months on a minesweeper, which came to her berth and flashed out a signal that warmed the cockles of every heart in the icy, North Russian air, 'Come over if you want your mail'. So they spent hours and hours, these seamen impoverished for news, reading and rereading news from home. Some had become fathers, uncles, grandfathers, even, in the time away from home on the grim Russian run.

Another great boost to the crew of *Harmatris,* as to all merchant seamen in Archangel, which came at this time of waiting for the homeward convoy, was the sudden presence of supplies of food, brought in by the allies, courtesy, among other agencies, of the NAAFI. Spirits rose. 'It's a lovely day tomorrow', as Vera Lynn sang in the song. Vera Lynn had graciously consented to be

Harmatris's mascot and special pin-up (and I'm sure that wasn't the only ship for which she acted in this capacity), and her picture was posted up all over the ship.

And so the growing need for food was catered for. Then there was coal, coal for those many ships in the convoys that burnt it. There was a massive, exhausting (it took days) coal-up.

Russian women came aboard *Harmatris* and other ships armed with shovels to trim the coal and send it hurtling down the chutes into bunkers. They were not very feminine-looking, poor girls, but they were hungry, and earned a few roubles for the job they did. As *Harmatris* provided them with the odd pot of soup, they did the job with great energy and gusto. There were no Russian men around who were not in the forces, wounded or elderly. And, for all that, Russian coal left a lot to be desired. Brundle wrote that at one point in convoy QP-14 he was forced to straggle behind the other ships due to the inferiority of Russian coal. Dust and earth: that's all much of the coal seemed to be. But that was all there was. And that's what they got, all 200 tons of it.

After the increase in food rations, after the bunkering with this inferior fuel, the crews of seamen thought they must be going soon. But rumour and counter-rumour prevailed. When you're waiting for something, when you're on the very edge of something, you become vulnerable to old Mother Rumour, and there are a few natural pessimists by temperament among the naturally incurable optimists, who keep the pot stirring.

Survivors taken on board merchant ships

What put the issue of the return convoy beyond doubt was that every ship of the convoy had to take on board a certain number of survivors. *Harmatris* took twenty; other merchantmen of similar size a similar number, anything from fifteen to thirty. Naval escorts were well loaded up.

PQ-18 and QP-14

The ships in the convoy were heavily escorted, in accordance with the current convoy strategy, which ran as follows. After

PQ-17, and the great losses it had sustained, the sailing of Arctic convoys to Russia was temporarily suspended. Now the plan was to fight a new convoy, PQ-18, through from Loch Ewe to Archangel, with fifteen fleet destroyers covering both this convoy, PQ-18, and a second convoy, QP-14, which was homeward-bound from Archangel. These two convoys, PQ-18, Russia-bound, and QP-14, UK-bound, would pass one another east and west of Bear Island.

PQ-18 sailed from Loch Ewe on 2 September 1942. Its escort was formidable and, as such an escort would do duty for QP-14 at the right time and place, they were divided into sections, a basic escort of the destroyers *Campbell, Eskdale, Farndale, Montrose, Walpole* and *Malcolm,* and the trawlers *Arab, Duncton, Hugh Walpole, King Sol* and *Paynter.*

At the Iceland rendezvous, reached on 7 September, those Western Approaches ships that had sailed from Loch Ewe with the convoy were relieved by ships that functioned as a close escort, the AA ships *Alynbank* and *Ulster Queen,* the destroyers *Achates* and *Malcolm,* the corvettes *Bergamot, Bluebell, Bryony* and *Camellia,* the minesweepers *Harrier, Gleaner* and *Sharpshooter,* the submarines *P-614* and *P-615* and the trawlers *Cape Argona, Cape Mariato, Daneman* and *St Kenan.*

The light carrier *Scylla* was a good and useful addition to this multi-layered escort force, which also included in the fighting destroyer screen *Ashanti, Eskimo, Faulknor, Fury, Impulsive, Intrepid, Marne, Meteor, Milne, Offa, Onslaught, Onslow, Opportune, Somali* and *Tartar.*

Fleet oilers were in attendance for such a large number of escorts, with three accompanying the convoy, and two remaining in readiness at Löwe Sound in Spitzbergen. Fuelling the ships took time, and emergencies could quickly develop.

The convoy PQ-18 was the subject of many attacks. Continually shadowed by BV 138 long-range spotter aircraft, the convoy was frequently under attack by He 111 torpedo-bombers or by Ju 88 bombers. It was an anxious and worrying time for both convoys. The security and effectiveness of PQ-18, their endurance and overcoming of difficulties ultimately meant security, effectiveness and safe harbour for QP-14, and all personnel in both convoys knew it.

A carrier and a CAM ship

The significant thing about PQ-18 (which was later to be transferred to QP-14) was the presence of the carrier HMS *Avenger*,
the first carrier to accompany a convoy to Russia. Three radar-
equipped Swordfish aircraft were on *Avenger's* decks for anti-
submarine work, and six Sea Hurricane fighters. Another six
were in pieces stowed beneath the deck, awaiting need. These
fighter aircraft came from 802 and 883 squadrons of the Fleet
Air Arm, while the Swordfish came from 825 Squadron. There
was another available Hurricane, to be flown from the CAM
(Catapult Aircraft Merchant) ship *Empire Morn*, the expendable
aircraft flown by the RAF's Merchant Fighter Unit. The aircraft,
if it should be needed, was to be flown by Flying Officer Burr.

The CAM ship was equipped with a catapult-like launching
device, so that one single Hurricane fighter could be catapulted
out. On completion of the flight, the pilot ditched in the sea, and
hoped to be picked up within two minutes. It was, needless to say,
a precarious existence. *Avenger* lost one of her Sea Hurricanes
from her deck. Steel ropes, strained beyond endurance, did not
stop aircraft escaping from their pens and crashing into one
another. More seriously the bombs, 500lb bombs, fused and
waiting, broke loose in the lift well and sailors in attendance had
to lay down duffel coats to recover them by means of rope ties
attached to the coats.

PQ-18 was harried from Iceland onwards. *Avenger* suffered
a near miss, while she was in Seidisfiord, from a stick of bombs
dropped by a Focke-Wulf Fw 200 Condor. No damage was
suffered, however.

Swordfish aircraft adopted the role of reconnaissance aircraft. They reported back to the convoy that they had seen
BV 138s dropping mines ahead of the convoy's path. When the
Sea Hurricanes were down on *Avenger's* deck, refuelling and
rearming, twenty-eight He 111s and eighteen Ju 88s made a low-
level torpedo attack, while a second wave of seventeen Ju 88s
swept in at almost mast-high level. Ignoring the escorts, the
attackers went for the merchant ships. That was their strategy
in convoy work. That was the strategy when those two enemy
aircraft attacked *Harmatris* outside the Kola inlet.

Eight ships were sunk, a devastating result. Loaded with high-explosives, the ammunition ship *Empire Stevenson* exploded taking one of the German aircraft with her.

An He 115, a Heinkel floatplane, was shot down when a number of them attacked. Eventually the captain of *Avenger* had to change his tactics with regard to the aircraft on his decks, as we shall see. The Germans, for their part, tried to force the Swordfish away from open flight by wheeling across the convoy and back over it. However, they were usually then hit by flak, and were driven away by the AA capability of the carrier and of the other ships.

Avenger was really hammered on 14 September in a mass attack by the Luftwaffe, as she moved at her maximum of 17 knots. Amazingly no ships were sunk, but the AA guns shot down eleven Ju 88s. Also another German aircraft was shot down, once again with no loss to the convoy.

Such amazing luck could not last. Although Commander Colthurst, in *Avenger*, managed, with success, to comb the torpedoes launched against him, the American ammunition ship *Mary Luckenbach* exploded from torpedo hits.

From the deck of HMS *Ulster Queen*, an AA cruiser, which was stationed to protect *Avenger*, the Chief Radio Operator saw it all:

> *As he passed* [an He 111], *a gunner raked him fore and aft and bright tongues of flame flickered from his starboard engine. He dipped, recovered, dipped again and seemed just about to crash, when his torpedoes reached their mark and the ship simply vanished into thin air. As for the plane, it broke up into small pieces.*

> (*Arctic Convoys 1941–1945*, Richard Woodman,
> John Murray 2004 pp. 274–275).

The only survivor from this cataclysmic explosion was a steward taking the Master a cup of coffee. The explosion blew him half a mile down the convoy. He was compelled by curious listeners to tell and retell this amazing story over and over again. Meanwhile, a rescue was effected by HMS *Offa*, one of the destroyers that came alongside the merchant vessel *Macbeth* when she was hit by two torpedoes and badly listing.

The next day, 15 September, Hurricanes and Swordfish were in the air again, when the Hurricanes were particularly successful at breaking up further Luftwaffe attacks.

On 16 September it was time for *Avenger* to leave PQ-18 and rendezvous with QP-14. She took all her aircraft with her.

A Sea Hurricane pilot, before the carrier departed, had been snatched from the sea minutes after baling out by another destroyer, *Wheatland*, also acting as close escort to *Avenger*. Flying Officer Burr, whose Hurricane was launched from the CAM ship, had managed to break up a German attack and set an aircraft on fire. Rather than ditch in the sea, after his ammunition was exhausted, he managed to save the Hurricane by flying it to an airfield near Archangel.

Brundle and his crew 'feel happy and ready for anything'

The other convoy, QP-14, was soon to cross with PQ-18. As they set out in it, Captain Brundle wrote that he and his crew felt 'happy and ready for anything'.

His mind must have been on his daughter's wedding in All Saints' Driffield the previous day, the day before QP-14 set out on Saturday, 12 September 1942. She on that day married her childhood sweetheart, Philip Wadsworth, a young Flight Sergeant in an operational squadron of Bomber Command. It was sad that Brundle couldn't be there to give his daughter away, but it was wartime. A family friend was standing in for him.

The special licence had been arranged, the wedding dresses made, and a telephone call made from RAF Elsham Wold to say that Saturday 12 September was to be the date. And yet on the Thursday, over Dusseldorf, the wedding plans almost came to nothing, as Philip Wadsworth's Halifax nearly collided with a Ju 88 over the target, and there was heavy flak and over 300 searchlights. So, on the wedding day, one of his fingers, grazed by a flak splinter, was bound up.

Brundle's mind must have been on all these things. In Driffield he was a member of the local Masonic Lodge, and the wedding reception was held in the Masonic Hall, with 130 guests attending.

Margaret and Philip Wadsworth were my mother and father. Sadly, after a tour with 103 Squadron on Halifaxes at Elsham Wold, my father's luck did not outlive the mounting losses of the time. On 27 April 1944 Flying Officer Philip Wadsworth, flying as flight engineer to the CO of 156 Pathfinder Squadron, was killed over Friedrichshafen, with all the rest of the Lancaster crew.

As Brundle watched the ships sail out into the Gourlo Strait and eventually the White Sea, he and the crew knew that there would be air attacks and U-boats, and the ever-present hazards of the weather. But that was infinitely preferable to languishing in Archangel or any of the other ports, without hope of any means of return home. They had survived so far, though some crew members had been ill, mainly due to the maddening privations and the irregularity of food provision. Now, however, all were fit to travel, and those who were slightly below par were buoyed up and empowered by the prospect of 'England, Home and Beauty'. Furthermore it was a different ship, and a different crew, with all these survivors on board.

QP-14 was full of ships carrying many seamen who, like the crew of *Harmatris*, had been in Murmansk and Archangel for several months. Included among those on the convoy's ships were many survivors from the ill-fated convoy PQ-17. This voyage, however, was to prove as hazardous for Brundle and his ship as the outward journey to Russia all those months ago. Although *Harmatris* this time did not become a casualty, Brundle and his ship were very near some of the actions which developed on this voyage, and close to some torpedoed ships. Commodore of convoy QP-14, on *Ocean Voice*, was Captain J.C. Dowding, an 'old hand' who had been Commodore of the very first convoy to Russia, codenamed 'Dervish', which had sailed from Hvalfiordur on 21 August 1941, and Commodore of PQ-17 as well, a fraught and unhappy experience.

Ocean Voice and *Ocean Freedom* were standard British ships, more than half-welded, like the classic Liberty ship, but constructed in the USA for British crews to sail in.

Empire Tide, also among the ships of the convoy, was a CAM ship. *Empire Byron*, another Empire Class ship, managed by J. & C. Harrison, Brundle's owners, had been sunk in PQ-17.

Formerly the Commodore ship of PQ-16, another recently contested and much-attacked convoy, *Ocean Voice* had had a huge hole torn in her side by bombs, not unlike the damage *Harmatris* sustained from Hackländer's torpedoes. But she survived the attack and was now taking part in QP-14 as the Commodore's ship, the lead ship. *Harmatris* was indeed in good company.

Ocean Freedom and *Ocean Voice* lead QP-14 out of Archangel

Sailing out of the Dvina Bar, and away from Archangel, convoy QP-14 settled into two columns, with *Ocean Freedom* leading one, and *Ocean Voice* leading the other. The Commodore ship, as already related, with the redoubtable Captain John Dowding, was *Ocean Voice*, with Captain Walker as Vice Commodore in *Ocean Freedom*.

Leading QP-14 out of the Dvina were the minesweepers *Britomart*, *Halcyon*, *Hazard* and *Salamander*. But not for long. Out of the Dvina these minesweepers detached, and another escort force took their place. *Leda* and *Seagull*, minesweepers, two Hunt Class Destroyers, *Blankney* and *Middleton*, AA ships, packed with AA armament, *Palomares* and *Pozarica*, the corvettes *Lotus*, *Poppy*, *Dianella* and *La Malouine* (fragrant names, but lethal to the U-boats, provided that they could stay upright in heavy storms) and the anti-submarine trawlers *Ayrshire*, *Lord Middleton* and *Northern Gem*.

In addition there was that force under Admiral Burnett, which included the cruiser HMS *Scylla*, the carrier HMS *Avenger*, and a force of destroyers. They were going to rendezvous with QP-14 in due course, after their duty of protecting PQ-18 had run its course.

Ships in QP-14

The other rescue ship, *Zaafaran*, had been sunk in PQ-17. Of the twenty ships in QP-14 nine were British and nine were American, with one ship, *Troubadour*, flying the Panamanian flag, and one Polish ship, SS *Tobruk*. From this point on there were more and more American ships making up the convoys.

One of the American ships, *Alcoa Banner*, was a member of a line of American ships that wrote their histories across the Murmansk and North Russian convoys, *Alcoa Cadet*, *Alcoa Rambler*, *Alcoa Ranger* and others.

The rescue ships *Zamalek* and *Rathlin* were in the convoy. *Zamalek* we last encountered in PQ-6, where she was detached from the convoy to help *Harmatris*. *Rathlin*, a small vessel of 1,600 GRT, had carried cattle on a run between Glasgow and Ireland. She was now transformed with medical orderlies, sick-bay attendants and so on.

The Samuel Chase and *Benjamin Harrison*: Liberty ships

Within the convoy's complement of American ships were two Liberty ships, which bore the illustrious names of signatories of the Declaration of Independence, *Samuel Chase* and *Benjamin Harrison*. Another two Liberty ships, which also bore the names of men who had signed the declaration, *John Witherspoon* and *William Hooper*, had been sent to the bottom in PQ-17. This constant reminder runs like a threnody throughout the telling of the names on the list of ships in QP-14, that sister ships, chummy ships, ships of the same class or category had met their end in that infamous, disastrous convoy.

The Liberty ships we are talking about here were 'Ugly Ducklings', built in record time. Both were of 7,191 GRT, and both were built that year, 1942. The building process was one of mass production at high speed, with pre-fabricated sections welded together instead of the handiwork for which Rosie the Riveter was responsible in the song current at the time. The time it took to construct a Liberty ship varied from forty-two days downwards. The fastest Liberty ship to be constructed around the time of our convoy, QP-14, was *Robert G Peary* (all were named after bona fide American heroes) which was launched from No. 2 shipway of the Permanente Metals Corporation of Richmond, California, on 12 November 1942, four days, fifteen hours and thirty minutes after the keel had been laid.

And so the rate of building of these Liberty ships rose above the rate at which the U-boats were sinking them, which is one of the main factors responsible for the allied victory in the Battle of the Atlantic. By 1943, the crucial year of the Atlantic battle, three Liberty ships were being built every day.

Survivors of PQ-17, men and ships

Some of the ships in QP-14 had on board PQ-17 survivors, a total of over 1,000 of them in the convoy. It was felt that, after such a catastrophe, much was riding on this convoy. Brundle and masters of other ships had taken on board extra men in the shape of survivors, and the conversation of these survivors was all about staying as survivors and going home. They were impressed, at least, at the very outset, with the level of escort, and increasingly impressed with this, as the escorts for PQ-18 trans-ferred their stations to QP-14. When they saw HMS *Avenger*, halfway through the convoy, they were more reassured as to their future, with the idea of an air component to their escort, while being prepared to join in the general merriment over the sight of one of the 'bathtub' carriers.

Not only were there over 1,000 men who had survived PQ-17 travelling in QP-14, but there were a number of entire ships that had survived making up the new convoy. Of QP-14's complement of twenty ships (nine American, nine British, one Panamanian and one Polish) ten had sailed before in PQ-17, five American, four British and one flying the Panamanian flag.

The American survivors of PQ-17 that sailed with QP-14 were USS *Samuel Chase, Benjamin Harrison, Bellingham, Silver Sword*, and *Winston Salem*; the four British ships were *Empire Tide, Ocean Freedom* and the rescue ships *Rathlin* and *Zamalek. Samuel Chase* and *Benjamin Harrison* were the brand-new Liberty ships built in American yards only a few months before PQ-17 set out. *Bellingham* had brought down a Focke-Wulf Condor that had attacked them in PQ-17, while *Silver Sword* on the same convoy had sought sanctuary with Lieutenant Gradwell in HMS *Ayrshire* after the command to scatter had been given, on the edge of the pack ice. Another ship that had sought safety and security on the edge of the ice was *Troubadour*, the Panamanian ship. This was a rather elderly tramp steamer, British-built in the 1920s, manned by diverse nationalities, who were near-mutinous when they learned that they were going to do the Russian run in

PQ-17. Her captain, a Norwegian, George Salveson, used a US Navy armed guard to quell a mutiny from twenty members of his own crew.

Winston Salem was another American ship that had had an eventful time in PQ-17. She had grounded on the coast of Novaya Zemlya, and, with Russian help, had to have some of the fuel pumped away from her to lighten her load, and effect her rescue and ultimately her passage to Archangel.

One of the British survivors of PQ-17, *Empire Tide*, a CAM ship, never used her Hurricane in anger in PQ-17, although it was fuelled up and made ready for launching. At least the sight of it scared off a high-altitude Ju 88.

There were two British fleet oilers sailing with QP-14, *Black Ranger* and *Gray Ranger*.

A BV 138 flying boat shadows QP-14

Moving from the White Sea to the Barents Sea, the convoy encountered a strong wind and choppy seas. Enemy attack was expected at any moment. But nothing happened yet. The crews of the convoy were on special alert when a Blohm und Voss flying boat acting as a 'spotter' aircraft and shadowing the convoy was noticed.

The BV 138 was ugly and slow-moving. Allied merchantmen, like characters out of Kipling, had pet names for everything. They called the BV 138 the 'Flying Clog'.

Looking up at the BV 138, the constantly shadowing aircraft, the seamen of the convoy were content to call it 'Charlie'. To the men of the convoy Charlie was the albatross of the Ancient Mariner. Certainly Charlie was like a bird of ill-omen, because, as he circled the convoy, he was constantly radioing to base details of the convoy and its position. And, as a result of those radio reports, the He 111s and the Ju 88s would soon be in evidence, not to mention the U-boats, clustering for the kill.

Because of the snow driving down on the convoy the seamen would only catch momentary glimpses of the spotter aircraft but it still managed to be so much in evidence that the crewmen developed a rather jokey approach to it. On a number of occasions, therefore, Charlie had actually had the audacity to radio the convoy for his position. Infinitely complicated and densely packed latitude and longitude bearings were then given, which, when assessed and interpreted, placed the German reconnaissance aircraft in the middle of the South Pacific. He really shouldn't have asked!

Another surviving story from this good-humoured banter with a deadly foe about to do incalculable harm to the ships of the convoy and their crews is the story of a signal sent by the Commodore of one convoy to Charlie, wearied, as he was, by the constant circling of the convoy by the aircraft: 'Please fly the other way round. You are making us dizzy.' And, unusual as this was in those times of war, Charlie had courteously acknowledged and turned the other way to continue his circling.

Depth-charge attacks were carried out by some of the escorting vessels, as U-boats had been reported off the southern tip of Spitzbergen. *Harmatris* lagged behind well astern of the convoy. She had a difficult time keeping station because of the inferior coal, a prediction that Brundle had made when coaling-up in Archangel.

HMS *Avenger*

During the early hours of 17 September the big escorts detached themselves from the eastward-bound PQ-18 to join the homeward-bound QP-14. There were forty warships, including seventeen destroyers, and the aircraft carrier HMS *Avenger*, with three Swordfish and twelve Hurricane aircraft. In popular parlance in the Royal Navy as well as in the Merchant Navy, *Avenger*, an escort carrier of the most basic kind was called a 'Woolworths' carrier. The 'Woolworths' designation came about as a result of its 'cheap and cheerful' quality. After all, *Avenger* was a cannibalised production, made out of a US merchantman's hull, with a rudimentary flight deck laid and welded and riveted in strips on top of this. It was always, and always would be the butt of good-humoured banter and jokes. From afar in the convoy it resembled a floating bath. Put a tap on it at either end and the transformation would be complete, opined the humorists among the convoy crews.

Contrast HMS *Avenger*, the very first carrier to sail in a convoy escort, with those legendary giants in the carrier world, those 35,000-ton ships like *Indefatigable* and *Illustrious*. Vessels like *Avenger*, which was of 12,850 tons, by contrast with them, were jokingly referred to as 'banana boats'.

Tragically, after furnishing much-needed help to the Arctic convoys in PQ-18 and QP-14, HMS *Avenger* was torpedoed and sunk in one of the actions connected with Operation Torch, the invasion of North Africa, on the night of 15 November 1942.

Avenger's tale is an interesting one, typical of wartime changes and chances. Originally launched in November 1940 as a motor passenger liner for the USA, she then bore the name *Rio Hudson* (shades of Bob Hope and the Road to Morocco). Nearly a year later she was loaned to the United Kingdom under the Lend-Lease programme, with all those old destroyers. Pennsylvania dockyard saw her renovation and conversion and unlikely metamorphosis into an auxiliary aircraft carrier for the Royal Navy. In March 1942 she was commissioned HMS *Avenger*. Leaving New York in a tanker convoy, she arrived at the Clyde in May 1942. All the time modifications were being completed, so that this erstwhile ugly duckling could become the true swan her planners and promoters could see was lurking beneath.

She had a vigorous first operation, escorting first PQ-18 and then QP-14, with her flight deck aircraft playing a distinguished part in the action of the two convoys. The 3 Swordfish aircraft she had aboard had flown, in the combined action of the two convoys, 32 sorties and carried out 6 out of 16 attacks on U-boats threatening the convoys. She had also 12 Sea Hurricanes on board, which had destroyed and damaged 26 aircraft in 31 combats during 59 sorties. In all, 42 German aircraft were destroyed.

HMS *Avenger*'s second and last operation was in support of Operation Torch, the allied landings in North Africa, as I said. As she was cruising west of Gibraltar and south of Cape St Vincent she ran into a pack (the Westwall group) of sixteen U-boats. Kapitänleutnant Adolf Piening, in *U-155*, sent out three torpedoes, one of which struck *Avenger*'s bomb room, an amazing target for any projectile to hit. It contained a formidable armament, thirty 500lb bombs, seventy 250lb bombs, a hundred and twenty 40lb bombs, and a hundred depth-charges.

The explosion blew out the centre of the ship, with bow and stern sections rising high in the air. The carrier sank rapidly, and was gone within three minutes. HMS *Glaisdale* found twelve survivors. Sixty-eight officers and 446 ratings perished. Among the 68 officers was the commanding officer, Commander Colthurst, who had played a sterling part in the actions of PQ-18 and QP-14. This was the heaviest British naval loss sustained in connection with Operation Torch.

Since her name had been changed from *Rio Hudson*, her short life had always been in the thick of the action. Her presence in PQ-18 and QP-14 was a first for a convoy escort. This is how her major contribution will be regarded, as that of pioneer. Had she not come to her untimely end, we would have seen her taking part in future convoys to Russia. Like so many of the ships chronicled here she now lies at peace beneath the ocean, 45 nautical miles south of Cape Santa Maria in Portugal.

'Stringbags' and chilblains

In PQ-18 and QP-14 the three Swordfish of HMS *Avenger* were fitted with radar for anti-submarine sorties. They kept the U-boats' heads down during crucial periods in the action of the convoys.

Avenger's commanding officer, Commander A.P. Colthurst, decided he must change his operating methods. He had released all his aircraft to tackle the German shadowers, so that, when the He 111s aimed with their torpedoes, there were no British aircraft in the skies. All had landed, and there was no fuel left. So he kept, in rotation, a number in the air almost all the time, not to chase after individual aircraft indiscriminately, thereby using up fuel, but to break up the bomber stream and deflect their purpose.

These open cockpits in the Swordfish aircraft induced a kind of loneliness, which mingled with the cold and the apprehension, and made the work of Swordfish air crew immensely draining and tiring. 'Oh, but it was cold flying in one of the "stringbags",' one of the Swordfish aircraft's pilots remarked, years afterwards, using the aircrews' nickname for them. He spoke of teeth chattering, and hands and feet chilblained.

They performed well, however, and in one all-out attack on 14 September by the Luftwaffe, KG 26 lost twenty aircraft and fourteen crews. Below the cloud level the enemy aircraft were subjected to a massive AA barrage, while above the cloud they met *Avenger's* fighters. Three German aircraft were shot down by AA fire during this all-out Luftwaffe attack.

Heavy snowstorms and that will-o'-the-wisp Arctic fog were encountered in the next stage of QP-14's progress, as her ships wove through massive, floating icebergs far up the Barents Sea. In the early hours of 17 September, the rendezvous with the mighty escort force of PQ-18 was effected, 17 destroyers, giving a total of almost 40 warships, escorting 14 merchantmen. For Brundle and the crew of *Harmatris* the cruiser *Scylla* was impressive enough, but what drew their eyes above all was that 'pudding basin' (this was one of the politest among the affectionate names) of a carrier, HMS *Avenger*. Inured to air attack as they were, the crew of *Harmatris* appreciated the presence of *Avenger*, and watched with rapt attention those Stringbags soaring slowly, ever so slowly, but inspirationally into the cold Arctic air, and setting a course for the south after circling the mother ship. It made them feel safe. They were aware too of the anti-U-boat work carried out by our aircraft, both Swordfish and Hurricanes, and, with the memory of three torpedoes, *Harmatris* was used to U-boat attacks.

In charge of the escorts of PQ-18, and now, of course, to do the same for QP-14 was the rear admiral in charge of Destroyers for the Home Fleet, Rear Admiral Bob Burnett, known to his many friends (he was an effective and popular senior officer) as 'Uncle Bob', and to those who held him in ungrudging affection for the way he could persuade anyone in the Navy to do anything for him, by the alternative soubriquet of 'Bullshit Bob'. He had his flag in the cruiser HMS *Scylla*.

HMS *Leda* and *Silver Sword* are sunk

The convoy was to have plenty of attention from both enemy aircraft and U-boats before they all reached their home ports, and the end of the voyage.

On 19 September from the deck of *Harmatris* Brundle saw the minesweeper HMS *Leda*, not far from him in the convoy, torpedoed. The ship was hit by two torpedoes, and took over an hour to sink. The captain, Commander Wynne-Edwards, and eighty-six of his crew were picked up, and accommodated aboard some of the merchant vessels and the rescue ships *Rathlin* and *Zamalek*. Sadly six died of wounds and hypothermia.

Later that day Brundle witnessed the sinking of an American steamer, *Silver Sword*, another U-boat victim. The ship's company were taken off in the difficult, turbulent seas, and HMS *Worcester* shelled her until she blew up, a sad end to one of the survivors of PQ-17.

The U-boat which put two torpedoes into HMS *Leda* was *U-435*, commanded by Kapitänleutnant Strelow. He had broken through the screen of the fighting destroyers and he would certainly go on to take advantage of his position, sinking another escort vessel, three merchant ships and a fleet oiler. Brundle stood by in *Harmatris* with nets for survivors but was just too far away, and was ordered to keep his place, and to maintain his station in the convoy.

The first he knew of *Silver Sword* being in trouble was the sight of a typical giant waterspout just by the bow of the vessel. As Brundle looked he saw a second waterspout leaping up near *Silver Sword*'s amidships. The escorts were quickly on her to pick up survivors. *Harmatris* was too far away to do that, and all Brundle's crew could do was stare impotently at the tragedy developing, and strive hard to keep *Harmatris*'s station in the convoy.

Fortunately *Silver Sword*'s demise did not turn into the slaughter it might have become. Nearly all hands were up amidships for their evening meal. One man, left in the quarters aft, was fatally injured and died during the night after the rescue.

HMS *Somali* is torpedoed

There was another ship torpedoed that day. This ship was HMS *Somali*, the Tribal Class destroyer that had escorted *Harmatris* in PQ-8 eight months before, and sister ship of the doomed *Matabele*.

The bulk of the men were seen off the decks and compartments of *Somali*, and her captain, Lieutenant Commander Maud, signalled that she might be saved if towed. The urge to save a ship, if at all reasonably possible, is something we witnessed in Brundle's case, with *Harmatris*, in January, outside the Kola inlet.

The seas were rolling and heavy, and the steel sections of which *Somali* was made groaned and complained bitterly above the noise of the wind and the screeching of the storm. Crewmen on *Somali* fought hard to plug gaps for the leaks with anything that was to hand.

HMS *Ashanti* acted as towing vessel to the crippled *Somali*. Nevertheless the severely damaged vessel could not maintain progress, and after an epic towing by *Ashanti* of 420 miles in eighty hours, the tow parted, and with a rending and collapsing of bulkheads *Somali* broke her back. *Ashanti* made all speed to pick up survivors, but, as *Somali*'s two halves sank, forty-seven men lost their lives.

Bellingham, Ocean Voice and *Gray Ranger* are sunk

The destruction and loss of life spread among the convoy like a contagion. On 22 September there was another dramatic loss of life with the torpedoing and sinking of another three ships, the American freighter *Bellingham*, the SS *Ocean Voice*, which was the ship of the Commodore, Captain John Dowding (who was saved with some of his crew), and one of the fleet oilers RFA *Gray Ranger*. This was a triple victory for Kapitänleutnant von Strelow, in *U-435*, and the third time Captain Dowding had had his ship sunk from under him. All the stricken ships had fallen victim to U-boats.

Avenger withdraws

The presence of the Swordfish biplanes obviously made a difference. Without them there might have been a carnage approximating to the scale of another PQ-17. And yet the crews of the Swordfish biplanes were utterly exhausted. After all, they had been with the sister convoy, PQ-18, right from the start. Consolidated Catalina flying boats from Sullom Voe in the Shetlands sought to plug the gap, when the 'Woolworths' carrier, HMS *Avenger* was forced to withdraw, now that QP-14 was beyond the range of massed attacks. By now, Brundle remarked in his report, giving a view from the deck of *Harmatris*, two Blohm und Voss flying boats were shadowing QP-14. Brundle saw a Catalina, after dropping its depth-charges, come down in the water. All the crew were taken off safely.

The Catalina was a Catalina III, 'Z' for zebra (FP525), of 330 Norwegian Squadron, flying from Akureyri in northern Iceland. The same aircraft had flown the first Catalina operation on 330 Squadron on 4 July 1942 with Lieutenant Abilsoe as pilot. The CO was Lieutenant Colonel Brinch. Most of the squadron were Norwegian, with the exception of a few aircrew and other squadron personnel, who were British.

Another Catalina sinks a U-boat

There was a notable Catalina success the next day, 23 September, which was witnessed by many of the seamen in the convoy. Catalina 'U' for uncle (FP115) piloted by Flight Sergeant J.W. Semmens, flying from Sullom Voe in the Shetlands and patrolling at 600 feet, astern of the convoy in some very rough weather, sighted QP-14 at about 06.00 hours. He retraced the steps of the convoy, as the foggy weather thickened around him. When he had just about given up patrolling this sector, he saw *U-253* less than a mile away.

The U-boat crash-dived, but Semmens was over it, almost at wavetop height, releasing six Mark VIII depth-charges into a troubled swirl of water, just as the U-boat was going under. There was a massive 'crump' detonation, causing a swelling in the water like a length of metal piping thrown 50 feet into the air. This blew the U-boat back to the surface. She wallowed for an instant, before dipping her snout vertically, plunging to her doom. The ten aircrew of U-for-uncle got a good view of the demise of the U-boat as the Catalina climbed away from the scene of the sinking, banking slowly.

It was to be the only patrol *U-253* had ever made. It was also the only patrol her captain, Kapitänleutnant Adolf Fredrichs, was ever to make. His boat, a Type VIIC U-boat was sunk with all hands.

Apart from the carrier HMS *Avenger*, there was the cruiser HMS *Scylla*, which carried the escort commander, Rear Admiral Bob Burnett. Having done her duty by the convoy, she had to leave them before they reached Loch Ewe, home and safety on 26 September.

Joint co-operation between PQ-18 and QP-14

This running of two convoys and planning and operating them jointly had been costly in terms of ships and seamen's lives. PQ-18, the eastbound convoy, had been a Pyrrhic victory, with the loss of 12 ships. QP-14 lost 3 merchantmen (*Silver Sword*, *Bellingham*, and *Ocean Voice*) and 3 escort vessels (HMS *Leda*, HMS *Somali* and RFA *Gray Ranger*). But the convoy had been 'fought through', German threats, after the overwhelming tragedy of PQ-17, had been defied, and vital equipment had been transported in the face of intensive attacks from the air and from U-boats.

This joint co-operation between PQ-18 and QP-14 was a strategy that worked. From the small convoy, PQ-8, in January to the larger and more complex QP-14 in September, with all the triumphs and tragedies between these dates lessons were being learned. Convoys would henceforth be 'fighting convoys', with close escorts, distributed, if possible, between an outward-bound and a homeward-bound convoy whose movements would be co-ordinated at all points. After convoy QP-15 a new code designation was used for the Russian convoys, JW for Russia-bound convoys and RA for returning convoys.

Loch Ewe, Tyne Dock and 'Home Sweet Home'

Brundle and the crew of *Harmatris* were relieved and thankful to have come safely through this last eventful convoy, having been almost grandstand observers of the mayhem and the slaughter being enacted all around them. At Loch Ewe, when it was reached, on 26 September, some 'Scotch' coal and fresh provisions were obtained, and Brundle was told to discharge at the wharf in Tyne Dock. He entered Tyne Dock and discharged the cargo on 4 October 1942.

Since he had set off from Port Glasgow on 27 November 1941, it had taken Brundle and his crew ten months to deliver his original cargo of military vehicles and equipment to Russia. Ten months enduring the misery and hopelessness of the North Russian ports, while ships were blown up and people died all round them. Although the owners and the Admiralty had striven to keep the families of the crew of *Harmatris* informed, news, at times, during this ten-month period was tardy in coming, and did not always get through. There was certainly a 'lost and found' feeling about the dedicated crew of *Harmatris*, and much rejoicing in their homes when they returned to them for a long leave, after coming into Loch Ewe with QP-14 and thence to Tyne Dock.

Tyne Dock, whither Brundle brought *Harmatris* on 4 October, is anything but beautiful, as compared with the Scottish beauty spots he had passed through, Loch Ewe and the Minches. But to the traveller making for home, after the ten months he and the crew had passed, it had its own special kind of beauty. For many of the Geordies in his crew this was home. For Brundle, negotiating the wartime trains from Newcastle to Hull and Driffield, with the waiting and security stops, and the vagaries of wartime travel, it was, in the words of the hymn, 'a day's march nearer home'. And so the long months of waiting, that feeling of being lost at the edge of the world, flashed by in a few hours, and Robert Brundle was with his own folk again. It was indeed a homecoming. Wartime food rations notwithstanding, they killed the fatted calf, in simple thankfulness and sheer rejoicing. The ice tundra of Murmansk had yielded him up. In the words of the Gospel parable he was lost, but was now found, was dead (often they feared so), but was now alive. After the responsibility of caring for a crew, extra passengers and a ship, on the hazardous return route, it must have been an incredible feeling to arrive at home for a good, long leave among those who loved and cherished him. From the nightmare world of Stalinist Russia, continually harried by the Ju 88s, to the warm safety of No. 5 Spellowgate, Driffield; it was indeed a healing of heart and mind, and to play the Russian metaphor, a kind of Tolstoyan resurrection.

CHAPTER 8

Other Ships, Other Convoys

Will no one tell me what she sings?
Perhaps the plaintive numbers flow
For old, unhappy, far-off things
And battles long ago.

'The Solitary Reaper',
Wordsworth (1807)

Tell me now, you Muses that live on Olympus, since you
are goddesses and witness all that happens, whereas we men
know nothing that we are told – tell me who were the captains
and chieftains of the Danaans. As for rank and file that came
to Ilium, I could not name or even count them, not if I had
ten tongues, ten mouths, a voice that could not tire, a heart
of bronze, unless you Muses of Olympus, Daughters of
aegis-bearing Zeus, would serve me as remembrances. Here
then are the captains of the fleet, and here are the ships from
first to last.

Homer: *The Iliad*, book 2, lines 484–493

Other convoys: the bigger picture

This chapter is an opportunity to pause, after my grandfather's homecoming and, while maintaining the focus on those two convoys, PQ-8 and QP-14, and what happened to the crew of *Harmatris* in between, to trace the background to the story through a look at other ships and other convoys and how they coped with their losses, relentless and devouring, which seemed to dog the footsteps of all seamen who took the Russian run until the very end of the war.

PQ-8 and other convoys

PQ-8, taken together with QP-14, is indeed the convoy war in microcosm. Consider the story of PQ-8.

It is the story of a small convoy of eight ships at the very beginning of the convoy process. It contains elements that are familiar to the Russian convoy story that we will find played out again in subsequent convoys, and which have a certain logic and momentum in our appreciation of the big picture of convoy identity and of convoy history. It also contains a number of firsts.

What are these elements? First a convoy of eight ships left Port Glasgow on the Clyde. Among the ships in PQ-8 was the American freighter *Larranga*, the first American ship, after Pearl Harbor, to sail under her own colours in a convoy to North Russia. *Larranga* was the vice commodore's ship. Thereafter the number of American ships in convoys assumed the proportions of a flood. Then there was a U-boat attack at the entrance to the Kola inlet, which was typical of an Arctic U-boat attack, one of the earliest such attacks in the tale of the convoys. The incident was a reflection of the carnage caused by U-boats on other, later convoys, more especially as *Harmatris* did not sink, but HMS *Matabele* did, with the loss of the entire ship's company except for two ratings.

This reflected the severe losses in a number of convoys, some of which we will touch upon, all of which needed to be heavily escorted. The demise of *Matabele* marked the first warship to be sunk on a convoy to Russia and looked forward to the escort carrier, and the presence of air power in a convoy (witness the presence of HMS *Avenger* in QP-14), which was in the end the only way to tackle the menace of the U-boats.

Meanwhile, Hackländer's second torpedo failed to explode, which is a factor to be examined in a moment.

Elements of the PQ-6 (where Brundle began) and PQ-8 stories include HMS *Edinburgh* and HMS *Trinidad* as escorts, and it is right to touch on their demise, just as we followed the fortunes of HMS *Somali*, another PQ-8 escort ship in the returning convoy QP-14.

HMS *Trinidad*'s all-welded hull was a 'first' for an escort ship in a convoy. She was not to be the last, but detached and on her own and preparing to go to the USA for specialised repairs, she fell victim to enemy aircraft and was sunk by Ju 88s and He 111s.

Speedwell's towing of *Harmatris* to Murmansk from a position outside the Kola inlet paralleled several such towings in a number of convoy battles, including HMS *Somali*, the longest such tow, in a dire emergency, on QP-14. *Speedwell*'s towing of *Harmatris* was another 'first', however. What became almost a commonplace in convoys, in the heat of enemy action, happened for the first time on this convoy. Indeed, PQ-8 almost set an agenda.

The attack by two aircraft on *Harmatris*, while this towing was going on, prefigured numerous air battles in PQ-18, QP-14 and other subsequent convoys, to be touched upon. For these two enemy aircraft, an He 111 and Ju 88, small beginnings though they may have been, were representatives of the coming of all those airfleets from North Norway and Finland to harry the convoys as they came into Murmansk. As the convoys continued, the Germans turned their attention momentarily from bombing and attacking them from the air outside the Kola inlet to bombing them while they lay in their berths in Murmansk, with cargoes undischarged. Several times during the fiery trials of Murmansk bombing raids Brundle felt that he was being singled out for attention when the bombs were falling. It is noteworthy that a number of other ships' masters felt the same.

The coming of air power to an escort of a convoy opened up the prospect of numerous air actions. Aircraft, even those apparently astonishingly frail-looking Swordfish, kept the heads of the U-boats down. Sometimes aircraft sank U-boats. A Sunderland sank Hackländer in *U-454* in August 1943, although the tenacious U-boat captain took the Sunderland with him. A Catalina flying boat sank another U-boat during the QP-14 convoy.

That was why the presence of the old Woolworths carrier, *Avenger*, in convoy QP-14 was so significant, and, indeed, life-changing, for it made the difference between whether men lived or died. In future, convoys got through because of air power, and, as this chapter shows, aircraft carriers were multiplied, to two or three carriers on some convoys, as well as cruisers, destroyers and all the rest. This got twenty ships through. This worked.

The earlier part of the convoy story, as far as the journey to the ports of North Russia is concerned, is one of destroyers and minesweepers, like *Matabele* and *Speedwell*, spending their lives dearly on behalf of a small convoy like PQ-8, in the belief that it must all get through, this cargo, these eight ships. It was all vital, with Russia under siege at the gates of Moscow and Leningrad. Every portion of an 8,000-ton cargo in the hold of a single ship mattered exceedingly. It must all get through.

Troubles with torpedoes

The significant factor on the other side, the amazing thing, is that it was the U-boats that continued, especially with their ever-developing technological improvements, to present a formidable challenge. Even in the early stages the scales were tipped in the direction of those U-boats. PQ-8 showed this, and but for the second torpedo sent by Hackländer failing to explode *Harmatris* might have had her toll of dead and wounded men. As it was Hackländer's torpedoes caused major damage to *Harmatris*; but loss of life was avoided.

But then faulty torpedoes were the negative side of the developing technology of U-boat weaponry. Look at what happened to HMS *Trinidad*, the 'ship that torpedoed itself'. The torpedo almost became Frankenstein's monster, to run and bite the hand that fed it as it did. Taking the antecedents of the torpedo right back, look at what happened to those early ventures in the field of torpedo technology, when Confederate and Union navies fought for supremacy on the banks of the Mississippi and Missouri rivers in the American Civil War. The outcome of this particular corner of the development of military technology was that torpedoes went on being faulty (the first phase of our story shows that a large number were) and torpedoes went on improving. The latest phase of torpedo development, the Gnat, with schnorkelling U-boats, is part of the same story. 'Gnat' was an acronym for German naval acoustic torpedo, as well as being a reference to the noise it made.

The Germans placed all their eggs in one basket. After the disappointing end of *Tirpitz*, it was U-boats, new and improved U-boats, with new and much improved torpedoes that were the dominant factor. The allies had developed air power to deal with the U-boat threat. They sometimes had as many as three carriers in a convoy. They put *Avenger*, the old 'banana boat', in PQ-18 and QP-14, and she was seen and blown up in her very next action. But the carrier remained the supreme resource. Even as cruisers, destroyers and minesweepers were becoming vulnerable, even expendable in the first phase of the story, in the second phase the carrier functioned as both normal weapon of offence, the home of Swordfish and Sea Hurricanes as well as being the convoy's Achilles' heel. When it came to grief, its ruin was very great, spectacular even, as we saw in the case of HMS *Avenger*, when she was sunk at the end of Operation Torch.

We can see, in this chapter, by taking our soundings throughout the entire convoy story, what astonishing developments were foreshadowed by the story of *Harmatris*, with her U-boat and air attacks, her being towed into the Kola inlet, her lying in wait at Murmansk, while ships were bombed and burned all around.

Like Ariadne's thread, the PQ-8 narrative contains clues from the long convoy story which recur later on in this same story. We keep on seeing the same vessels which figure dramatically in the tale of PQ-8 later on in the encounters of ships in a convoy. We may be present at their demise. They are our tools for understanding the logic and direction of the convoy story.

PQ-17 was the supreme, the ultimate disaster. And yet the tale of the Russian convoys was not plain sailing either before or after PQ-17 and its disastrous consequence. Many convoys made the whole distance along that terrible route, only to be jumped by a U-boat at Kildin Island, or blown up at an overcrowded berth in Murmansk, barely after arrival, while their valuable cargo was still waiting to be discharged.

Vast quantities of material shipped to Russia from Britain

Britain between October 1941 and March 1946 shipped to the USSR war material valued at £308 million. Foodstuffs and medical supplies shipped to Russia came to £120 million.

The war material Britain shipped over comprised 5,218 tanks, 7,411 aircraft, 4,932 anti-tank guns, 4,000 rifles and machine-guns, and naval vessels amounting to 9 torpedo aircraft, 4 submarines, 14 minesweepers, 10 destroyers and a battleship. All this came by the North route, the Russian run. The allies (notably the USA) also delivered to Russia 2,000 locomotives, 11,155 railway wagons, as well as steel rails. Among the American shipments were included 15 million pairs of boots! The total value of the American shipments was $11,260,343,603. Of the American shipments a quarter came via the Arctic route, a quarter via the Persian Gulf, and half by way of the Pacific.

'Moments' in the convoy war

This was the material Britain shipped to Russia on the run to Murmansk and Archangel.

We look now at some moments in the convoy war, making comparisons all the way with the story of PQ-8, and first we look at those convoys and activities that spelled out the loss of HMS *Edinburgh* and *Trinidad*.

When convoy PQ-6 arrived in Murmansk in December 1941 it was with HMS *Edinburgh* acting as escort. It is to *Edinburgh* and her sister cruiser, *Trinidad*, that we turn now to look at their last sailings in convoy. *Trinidad*, you remember, escorted PQ-8 to Murmansk with Brundle and *Harmatris*. In January 1942 both these cruisers played a part in the story of *Harmatris*. The tales of their last voyages and actions complete the drama of convoys PQ-6 and PQ-8, and we follow the action right up to the sinking of these two cruisers.

HMS *Edinburgh*

We look at *Edinburgh* first, as *Edinburgh* was the first to go. One hundred and fifty miles from Bear Island, QP-11, which had left the Kola inlet on 28 April 1942, was being attacked by six Ju 88s.

The convoy was rapidly to become a focus of trouble, with four German destroyers attacking it. Operating close to the convoy was the cruiser HMS *Edinburgh*, now badly damaged, and horribly destroyed in a torpedo attack. Her hull was twisted, and there was a consequent loss of power in the damaged area, which put pressure on numerous frightened men, who could not see or discern the escape routes. Rear Admiral Bonham-Carter had his flag on the cruiser, and the captain was Captain W.H. Faulkner.

There was another factor in play for the stricken *Edinburgh*. In one of her magazines were secreted five tons of Russian gold bullion (worth about £59,000,000), which was in transit to the United States Treasury, as part-payment for the munitions and material coming from the USA on these convoys. They had loaded the gold on the ship at Vaenga, with an unusually heavy armed guard of Russian soldiers, and allied marines. One rating, labouring with heavy bullion boxes, uttered a Cassandra-like prophecy to an officer supervising the loading: 'This will be a bad trip, Sir. This is Russian gold, and it's dripping with blood.' As a prophecy this was chillingly accurate, with the cries of trapped men, and men wounded and dying ringing round the ship when she was attacked.

Admiral and Captain determined to try to save the ship. The damaged areas were sealed off, and *Edinburgh* was able to steam ahead at 8 knots, notwithstanding the uncomfortable fact that her bow was down in the water. But she could not be steered.

The destroyer *Forrester*, sailing nearby, got a line aboard to provide steering by taking the cruiser's anchor chain. Four times she tried to do this, and four times the attempts were futile, and the crew slithered and slipped on the decks, encrusted as they were with ice.

Forrester had to break off this series of attempts to attack a U-boat which had just come to the surface. After this she did get a line through the destroyer's bull-ring. The Russian destroyers also protecting *Edinburgh* announced that they were short of fuel, and so had to leave.

Remaining destroyers in the vicinity were asked to provide a screen for *Edinburgh* against U-boats, while Admiral Bevan, the SBNONR, organised a Russian patrol vessel to stand close to *Edinburgh*. Later, at midnight 1/2 May, a tug and a minesweeper joined *Edinburgh*. With the help of the total of four minesweepers now escorting her, *Edinburgh* was towed, with some difficulty, at a speed of 3 knots.

The German destroyers, meanwhile, kept firing in the direction of *Edinburgh*.

Destroyers and minesweepers defended her 'like three young terriers, going in and firing when they could'. The cruiser was by now totally out of control and slowly circled the action, unable to bring her guns to bear, and conversely unable to present a stable target for the enemy to hit.

An examination of *Edinburgh* by Captain Faulkner and his engineer officer indicated strongly that the ship, being completely open to the sea amidships on both sides, might break her back at any moment. Bonham-Carter ordered the ocean minesweeper *Gossamer* alongside to take off the wounded and Merchant Navy personnel whose ships had been sunk on the way to North Russia.

The destroyer screen had defended *Edinburgh* valiantly. *Forrester*, after firing three torpedoes at the German destroyers, had a salvo of shells fired at her, which struck her and killed her commanding officer, Lieutenant Commander Huddart, and wrecked a part of the ship. Soon *Edinburgh* herself was hit and the evacuation of crew and other personnel began; 450 officers and men were being transferred to *Gossamer*. All the while this was going on, B turret of *Edinburgh* continued to fire, until the ship's listing reached a dangerous 17 degrees, so that guns could not be brought to bear on their target and the guns had to be silent.

Bonham-Carter ordered Captain Faulkner to abandon ship. HMS *Harrier* took off these two senior officers, and the rest, some 350 officers and men.

As his final act Bonham-Carter gave instructions for *Edinburgh* to be sunk with a torpedo. In an almost leisurely fashion, she disappeared beneath the water.

Trinidad

Trinidad, the light cruiser which had escorted *Harmatris* and the rest of PQ-8 to Murmansk, was engaged as a cruiser providing close escort to convoy PQ-13. PQ-13, comprising twenty-one ships of several nationalities, leaving Loch Ewe on 10 March 1942, had a troubled time in transit, and was exposed to the attention of the Luftwaffe on arrival in Murmansk. An attempt was made to synchronise the movements of the PQ- convoy with those of the QP- convoy, although QP-9, the homeward-bound convoy sharing escorts with PQ-13, was delayed by U-boats on the environs of the Kola inlet, the most vulnerable focus of any convoy, Russia-bound or homeward-bound. There was in the ranks of PQ-13 another J. & C. Harrison ship, another merchantman well known to Brundle, at that time undergoing his enforced stay in Murmansk. This ship was *Harpalion* (note the initial letters of the ship's name, 'Ha').

It was also one of the merchant ships to be sunk on this convoy of PQ-13, although all her crew were taken off. Brundle knew the ship's Master and saw the survivors of this convoy in the crews of other ships, limping to their berths in Murmansk, with the terrible damage they had sustained. He was there in Murmansk on the quay when the battered and damaged ships came in. He watched the troubling panorama unfold.

More than a quarter of the cargoes of the ships of PQ-13 combined had been sunk, including the one carried by *Harpalion*, when the surviving ships of the convoy arrived in Murmansk harbour. While PQ-13 was in progress, and HMS *Trinidad* was one of the escorts, German destroyers attacked the escorts. HMS *Trinidad* and HMS *Fury* were in the thick of duels with German destroyers. A German destroyer, *Z-26*, struck with a shell *Trinidad*'s aft 'Y' turret, while *Trinidad*'s own fire hit *Z-26* amidships.

Another two German destroyers started evasive manoeuvres. *Trinidad*'s torpedo officer launched her first torpedo at *Z-26*, only to see it, with horror, promptly reversing course and making its way back to *Trinidad*, to crash into the port side.

Trinidad became known after this as the 'ship that torpedoed itself'. It was a stroke of 'cruel, hard luck', as Admiral Tovey called it. The severe Arctic conditions caused a failure of the gyro-controlled direction system, causing the torpedo to stop dead in its tracks and then reverse its course. The reversed torpedo took its own quota of damage on the ship and of loss of life, with men in the boiler room scalded as they sought frantically and uselessly to get out.

Meanwhile, *Eclipse*, another destroyer, fought a duel with her German counterpart, Z-26, and ultimately sank her.

On 28 March minesweepers from the Kola inlet came out to look for survivors of PQ-13 and for ships in trouble. The crippled *Trinidad* was in a bad way. She had developed an alarming list, and efforts were made to alleviate this by transferring fuel between the ship's tanks. Men were still trying to escape from difficult and dangerous situations in the ship, and a few were scalded in the forward boiler room.

Help and relief was found for all those in distress, and *Trinidad* was enabled to enter the Kola inlet on 30 March. Later, on 13 May, *Trinidad* left to go to Iceland and thence to the USA for more permanent and enduring repairs. *Trinidad* had an all-welded hull, and American shipyards could deal with this more expertly than British shipyards.

On the way to Iceland *Trinidad* was attacked by Ju 88 dive-bombers. She had been roughly welded in Murmansk, and under the strain of the firing of the guns and the evasive action, she groaned and shook. The Ju 88s were joined by He 111s.

And then the inevitable happened. While she was turning to port to evade the torpedoes to starboard from the He 111s, four bombs from the Ju 88s were dropped on the cruiser. A first bomb, although it nearly landed in the water, tore off some steel plating, and water entered the ship, engulfing the magazine. The second bomb tore a big hole in the port side, exploding in the mess decks of stokers and petty officers. The two final bombs were damaging near-misses. The inadequate temporary welding done at Murmansk gave way under pressure, and water forced itself into the vessel.

So *Trinidad* burnt fiercely, and took in water. She still fought on, nevertheless, until it became necessary to abandon ship.

Matchless, Forrester, Foresight and *Somali* took all who were able to leave *Trinidad* off. On board *Somali* Rear Admiral Bonham-Carter ordered *Matchless* to sink *Trinidad* by sending three torpedoes into her starboard side, so that the end came on 15 May 1942 at 01.20 hours. Bonham-Carter mentioned to some survivors, as he was being taken off *Trinidad*, that he was becoming something of a Jonah, as he had had five ships sunk from under him.

After these experiences, and in view of the plight of many merchant seamen, as well as RN personnel in the escorts, Bonham-Carter wrote to the Commander in Chief, Home Fleet:

> *We in the Navy are paid to do this sort of job, but it is beginning to ask too much of the men of the Merchant Navy. We may be able to avoid bombs or torpedoes with our speed, a six or eight knot ship has not this advantage.*

The end of HMS *Trinidad* was the end of the light cruiser which escorted *Harmatris* in PQ-8. At the time this was a new venture, for a convoy to be escorted by a light cruiser with an all-welded hull. The Admiralty, two or three months before, at the time of PQ-8's experience, were convinced that American welded ships were not tough enough, compared with all-riveted constructions, to withstand the depredations of the Arctic weather and Arctic conditions.

American zeal and Russian luke-warmness

Admiral Tovey, prompted by Bonham-Carter and others, did his best to influence Churchill to suspend the Russian convoys during the long summer days. Churchill was adamant, however, that the convoys must go through, summer and winter alike, and Roosevelt also was implacable on this issue, and, as an earnest act of his good faith, sent a squadron of American ships to join the Home Fleet of the Royal Navy. And so the battleship USS *Washington* (with her 16-inch guns), the carrier *Wasp*, two heavy cruisers, *Tuscaloosa* and *Wichita*, together with six destroyers, commanded by Rear Admiral R.C. Griffen, sailed with the convoys. From now on every convoy to Russia had a greater proportion of American merchant ships than previously. *Larranga*, the American freighter of the vice commodore accompanying Brundle in PQ-8 was the very beginning of the process. For it was a 'first': the first American ship in a convoy to Russia, after Pearl Harbor, flying her own flag.

Look at how this trend developed, and at the large number of American vessels present in the infamous and ill-fated convoy PQ-17.

The oft-heard complaint of the convoy men, whether merchant seamen or Royal Navy, was about the total lack of responsibility for any convoy, often hard-fought, evinced by the Soviet Navy. The Germans had sown mines around the approaches to the Kola inlet, and those Soviet escorts that did join an incoming or outgoing convoy only accompanied the vessels for a short distance before returning. This kind of 'semi-detached' involvement in the naval war was astonishing to allied seamen, who knew, especially after the successful denouement of the Stalingrad offensive, that the Red Army could and did fight like tigers, and who knew also that, wherever Russian ships were involved in any convoy, the crew quite often acquitted themselves magnificently. This behaviour of studied withdrawal was almost a conscious policy of setting distance between the Russians and the allies, as if to say: 'The convoys are yours. The real fighting on the soil of Mother Russia is ours. This one is Churchill's war. The other is Ivan's war.' But sometimes, as we have seen, the two did meet.

Demise of some Harrison ships

As he waited in Murmansk and saw damaged ships come in, Brundle thought about other ships owned by J. & C. Harrison of London, ships whose masters and officers he knew, which had been affected by the mounting casualties of the time. For one after the other the Harrison ships were going. There was the news about the sinking of *Harpagus* in May 1941, which came to Brundle before the convoys PQ-6 and PQ-8. The Master of *Harpagus*, Captain J.V. Stewart, on an Atlantic convoy had hove *Harpagus* to in order to rescue and recover Captain T.A. Robertson of

Norman Monarch. He had been attacked by a U-boat in convoy HX-126. Lost with *Harpagus* was Robertson, with 19 of his crew and all 6 of his DEMS naval gunners; as far as *Harpagus* and Captain Stewart were concerned, 25 crew, 3 passengers, and 4 gunners were killed.

Brundle remembered *Harpagus* when he was a young ship's Master, in happier times, in peacetime, and trips ashore with officers and ratings mingling indiscriminately, and that little lascar at the end of the row in the tell-tale photograph, who was their mascot and seemed to look after them all.

Then there was the sinking of *Harpalion* in March 1942 in convoy PQ-13, the convoy of which *Trinidad* was an escort, and, the loss of *Hartlebury* in PQ-17 in July 1942, which resulted in loss of life, and ultimately in the death of Captain Stephenson from the wound to his head.

Finally there was *Empire Byron*, which J. & C. Harrison managed. She had been lost in PQ-17, and, after some loss of life, her Master (Captain Wharton) and some of her crew had been rescued.

As Brundle reflected in Archangel, on the eve of taking the ship back to the UK in QP-14, he was immensely grateful for the steady and unfeigned loyalty and reliability of officers and crew. The journey back, with *Harmatris*, packed to the gunwales with PQ-17 refugees, would demand such loyalty, such reliability. For it was not, Brundle mused, going to be an easy or straightforward journey. Silently he prayed they would all come through it.

QP-15 and *Goolistan*

Most convoys sustained some casualties. It became unusual to arrive at either the Kola inlet or Loch Ewe without having lost one ship or more. QP-15, a homeward-bound convoy, which left Archangel on 17 November, nearly made the trip without casualties, only for one merchantman in the convoy, the SS *Goolistan*, to be sunk with the loss of all forty-two hands. This convoy was to be the last in the PQ-/QP- series. The next one would be coded JW-51A, and the next homeward-bound convoy RA-51.

The Battle of the Barents Sea

There were some convoys, on the other hand, which turned into major fleet actions. What was called the Battle of the Barents Sea centred round the protection of convoy JW-51B. It was a very bloody affair indeed, and ended on 3 January 1943. Captain Sherbrooke, in charge of the destroyer escorts, was badly wounded, and was awarded the VC. Five destroyers held off an enemy force of at least one pocket battleship, one heavy cruiser and six destroyers for four hours, and drove them off without any loss to the convoy. In a self-sacrificial attempt to save the convoy HMS *Achates* and HMS *Bramble* remained fighting to the last, with guns firing even as they were sinking. They 'engaged the enemy (ever) more closely' in the very best traditions of the Royal Navy.

The Battle of North Cape: *Scharnhorst* at sea

Nearly a year later another admiral, Admiral Fraser, and his staff on HMS *Duke of York* received a signal on Boxing Day 1943: 'ADMIRALTY APPRECIATE THAT SCHARNHORST IS NOW AT SEA.' The 'battle' of the North Cape was fought around convoys JW-55B and RA-55A. Admiral Sir Bruce Fraser and his staff were on his flagship, *Duke of York*, while Vice Admiral Sir Robert Burnett was in command of the cruiser squadron from his flag on the cruiser HMS *Belfast*. A fierce gale and Arctic storm raged throughout the action, which prevented the convoy from altering course and hence from steering into the predatory and menacing attentions of *Scharnhorst*. Attacked on all sides by guns and torpedoes, *Scharnhorst* was sunk. It was to save the convoy, this fleet action; it was not an end in itself, but *Scharnhorst* was sunk, with the loss of 1,767 officers and ratings.

After those two actions, the 'battles' of the Barents Sea and of North Cape, the days of heavy surface ships slogging it out, even to protect the convoy, were over and gone. Convoys needed a considerable number of escort ships. The process began with PQ-18 and QP-14, on which Brundle made his return journey in September 1942. The result of this is that escort ships of convoys fought sea battles with German surface ships, celebrated ships like *Lützow*, *Hipper* and *Scharnhorst*. *Tirpitz*, for deep atavistic reasons that lodged in the brain of Hitler, was, as we shall see, always being withdrawn from the fight.

After the North Cape action, however, convoys never again became bait for the big ships, and Hitler wasted the potential of his surface fleet languishing in the fiords of North Norway. Hitler was, for some reason, paranoid about Norway as a potential focus for future British action. As a result he reined-in his ships whose legendary names struck terror into the hearts of allied seamen, both merchantmen and escorts. Hitler's views caused mayhem in the Kriegsmarine, when he threatened to do away with the surface fleet. They caused the resignation of Admiral Raeder, and much else besides.

Schnorkel and Gnat

The rest of the convoy story, however, was still bleak in the telling. It was to remain so to the bitter end.

U-boats made killings to the end of the war, a potential which was, in fact, enhanced by development and improvements in U-boat design and construction, such as the so-called Schnorkel, which enabled a U-boat to use her diesel engine at periscope depth, and the T-5 acoustic torpedo (the German Naval acoustic torpedo), named by the allies the Gnat, which homed in on the noise of a ship's propeller.

The German 'schnorkel' and the Gnat – the T-5 acoustic torpedo – were more than mere irritants to the allied cause. On a number of occasions they almost tipped the balance in favour of the Germans, causing considerable damage to a convoy, and the sinking of a good proportion of the cargo for Russia. There was never again to be another PQ-17. No one was going to take such actions on the basis of mistaken intelligence reports. The Admiralty would never again command a convoy to scatter. But a string of convoys with significant losses might well cause the allies to revise their tactics. And it was a fact that, as the tide of war turned in favour of the Russians, the USSR needed more than ever the tons of equipment that continued to be sent to her via the Russian run.

American-built tanks and military vehicles were particularly sought after, and their presence in the arsenal of the USSR, as she pushed on towards victory, was an indelible part of the total strategy. Never at any time would Russian convoys become a sinecure, a milk run. They were always dangerous, always attacked by the Germans, always harassed by the weather.

JW-59

The story of convoy JW-59, which left Loch Ewe on 15 August 1944, is an instructive lesson in the combating of these new U-boat developments. It had a heavy escort of two carriers, and put all the weight of its resources on seeing the convoy to a safe arrival and on combating the U-boats.

JW-59 comprised three tankers, *British Promise*, *Lucullus* and a Norwegian tanker, *Herbrand*, with the last two additionally acting as oilers, the rescue ship *Rathlin* (the good little *Rathlin*, a former cattle carrier), and another thirteen British ships, nine of which were Liberty ships.

These British-manned Liberty ships were oil-fired, with midships accommodation and funnel. The 'sam' prefix which distinguished their names had nothing to do with Uncle Sam but with the MOWT, who described them, in technical terms, as 'Superstructure Aft of Midships types'. The Commodore, G.H. Creswell, had his place in one of these SAMs, *Samtredy*. *Samsuva* which sailed in JW-59, and *Samaritan*, which sailed in JW-60, had the most felicitous name in the entire bunch were other examples of the type, of which there were 200 in existence.

This convoy was distinguished by a number of changes in its composition, which, together with the way its story unfolds, is why it is worthy of our consideration, and why it highlights the progress and development of the Russian convoy story. JW-59 was a far cry from PQ-8, but remember that the story goes via QP-14, the seminal convoy for future developments. There were two carriers. *Vindex* had a rear admiral and his flag, Rear Admiral Dalrymple-Hamilton, and operated twelve Swordfish; the other carrier, *Striker*, operated twelve Avengers and six Wildcats. In addition to these two carriers there was a cruiser, *Jamaica*.

There was a close escort of corvettes, *Bluebell, Camellia, Charlock, Honeysuckle* and *Oxlip,* fragrant names to bear for ships with the deadly business of being superb submarine chasers. There was a sloop, *Cygnet,* a frigate, *Loch Dunvegan,* and the destroyer *Whitehall.*

Ten miles out on the left rear flank of the convoy were the frigates *Mermaid* and *Peacock,* with *Keppel* and *Kite* on the right, and a spread of destroyers ahead of the convoy, *Caprice, Milne, Marne, Meteor* and *Musketeer,* who joined from Scapa Flow. There was, in addition, a Russian element with them, the former British battleship *Royal Sovereign,* now called *Archangelsk* (the British called her the 'Regal Rouble') and eight of the original fifty four-stack American destroyers ceded to Britain under the Lend-Lease agreement.

A five-strong wolfpack harried the convoy, sinking Lieutenant Commander A.N.G. Campbell's *Kite,* with only nine men being saved by *Keppel,* although *Mermaid* tried to assist and counter-attack, before she was recalled.

Air patrols from *Vindex* and *Striker* kept the heads of the U-boats down, and *U-344* was bombed and sunk by a Swordfish from 825 Squadron from the deck of *Vindex.*

All enemy submarines were using the T-5 acoustic torpedo, the Gnat, against the enemy and elsewhere. To counter the acoustic torpedoes British ships were equipped with a towed device called the 'foxer'. Trailing in the ship's wake, it sent out a countering noise on which the Gnat homed and was detonated harmlessly astern. The price the allies paid for such a counter device was a loss of sharp effectiveness in their Asdic equipment. The Gnat detonated at the pseudo-noise, but this sometimes led to loss of contact with the echo, which was the very principle behind sonar Asdic.

Sometimes German T-5 acoustic torpedoes detonated prematurely, as happened in the unfolding of the drama of this convoy, where *U-711* fired T-5s at *Archangelsk* and *Zharki,* and when the T-5 detonated prematurely and harmlessly without the Russians having any working countermeasure to deal with it.

The remaining two U-boats that were in a position to attack were now hunted by *Keppel, Peacock* and *Mermaid.* Lieutenant Commander Mosse of *Mermaid* suddenly heard a significant

Asdic ping, and took anti-Gnat precautions only just in time. Precisely ninety seconds later a Gnat exploded close astern, and a minute later another.

Destruction of a U-boat

A depth-charge attack was launched but it failed to locate the U-boat. The crew of *Mermaid* saw a conning tower astern of where they were surfaced briefly. Mosse of *Mermaid* went in chase, after the U-boat dived. *Loch Dunvegan* launched a squid attack, but her Asdic set broke down. *Mermaid*'s third attack was the best of all the actions of the two ships hunting the U-boats. The depth-charges set up a leak in the U-boat's tanks which caused a leak of diesel oil 5 miles long and 1 mile wide.

Rear Admiral Dalrymple-Hamilton wanted to recall Mosse, but Mosse counter-argued 'the depth of water was hardly sufficient to burst the hull [of the U-boat] if he was lying on the bottom'. Mosse's senior officer, Wigley, gave him all the latitude, and after the deadline was extended twice more, with *Keppel* and *Peacock* joining in the hunt, Mosse left the U-boat gushing oil and severely damaged. In the Admiralty report Lieutenant Commander Mosse was praised: 'a grand story of pertinacity ... There is no moss on Mosse'.

JW-59 arrives in the Kola inlet: Lieutenant Commander Mosse 'kills' another U-boat in convoy RA-59A

JW-59 arrived in the Kola inlet on 25 August 1944, after an eventful convoy. Escorts had losses, with two frigates sunk, but a U-boat had been destroyed, several damaged, and the convoy had got through. In PQ-17 there were no casualties among the escorts, but 153 merchant seamen had perished, and two-thirds of the convoy of merchant ships had been sunk. By contrast, this convoy, JW-59, signalled a return to the sharp end and a cost for convoy protection, as it was in the old days in PQ-8, with Brundle and *Harmatris*, when *Matabele* was sunk protecting the convoy, when escort vessels gave their lives to protect the convoy and to see it got through.

Mosse, the captain of *Mermaid*, having destroyed one U-boat on JW-59, destroyed another on the return convoy, RA-59A. It was essentially a small convoy, five ships from JW-58, sailing on 28 August, *Barbara Frietchie*, *Empire Prowess*, *Fort Vercheres*, *Lacklan* and *W.R. Grace*. In addition there were the extremely useful heavy-lift ships *Empire Bard* and *Empire Elgar*.

A Swordfish patrolling from the deck of *Vindex* came upon a U-boat on the surface of the sea. She was recharging her batteries. The convoy's support group of escort ships recorded the position the Swordfish was maintaining with a smoke marker, before she crash-dived. Contact had been lost, however. Suddenly, both *Mermaid* and *Peacock* received Asdic responses. *Peacock* made a patterned depth-charge attack but, taking time to sink, the U-boat evaded these by deducing time and distance from Asdic pulses and the noise of propellers, and taking suitable evasive action.

The next expedient was to carry out the 'creeping attack', so beloved of Captain Johnnie Walker, its 'onlie begetter', and his anti-submarine officer, Michael Impey. To keep down any extraneous noise they recovered and removed those trailing and towed devices known as 'foxers'. *Mermaid* had the central position of the creeping box of ships, with *Keppel* slightly to port, and *Whitehall* to starboard. All three turned off, and forbore to use their Asdics, slowing down to 7 knots. The only ship to maintain Asdic contact was *Peacock*, astern of the line, and as the master ship in the plan, she directed the movements of the other three warships in front of her. When *Peacock*'s Asdic operations judged that the group of three were over or on top of the enemy, then they attacked, with *Keppel* throwing 22 depth-charges to port, *Whitehall* 22 to starboard and *Mermaid* rolling 18 over the stern. So the U-boat was caught in a kind of depth-charge cross-fire, all set to detonate at between 350 and 900 feet.

Mermaid's Asdic registered three big underwater explosions, and Mosse, as ever, persistent, moved in for a final attack, which was probably unnecessary. There were on the surface bubbles and flotsam, and human remains which the naval surgeon on *Peacock* classified as being of blood group four. *U-394* had undoubtedly imploded under the impact of multiple exploding depth-charges. Her captain, Kapitänleutnant Wolfgang Borger, and crew all perished. The U-boat war, like the entire convoy war was a bloody and relentless affair. The escorts had to kill the U-boats in this thoroughgoing fashion to protect the ships in the convoy. RA-59A arrived safely at Loch Ewe on 6 September 1944.

JW-61

Different phases of war generated different enthusiasms. Towards the end of 1944 Churchill and the Royal Navy were yearning for the Pacific and for a substantial British naval presence there to take on the Japanese. And yet the British presence in northern and eastern coastal naval bases was considerable, and just one Arctic convoy JW-61, sailing from Loch Ewe at a late stage in the war, on 20 October 1944, was thought to have the need for three carriers among the escorts, one cruiser, seven destroyers, twelve escort destroyers, two sloops and three corvettes.

Once again it is instructive to trace, at least in outline, the fortunes of this convoy, as a means of assessing the progress and development of the Arctic convoy story from the early PQ-series onwards. In this enquiry Brundle's convoy, PQ-8, is seen, like the god Janus, to face both ways: PQ-8 faces back towards the early convoys and towards the tentative beginnings of the Russian convoy system, and it faces forward to the massive return convoy, QP-14, which shared its fighting escort with PQ-18. It does this because of what befell *Harmatris* and *Matabele*, because theirs, in those early months of the convoy process, was a watershed experience. But PQ-8 also looks further on towards the end of the story, to a time when, despite allied air and sea supremacy, the U-boats, possessed of Schnorkel and the T-5 acoustic torpedo, were a powerful and prolonged threat, especially to the later convoys, even when two or sometimes three carriers were present. This partial story of a mere handful of those later convoys, therefore, will help us to put PQ-8 in perspective. To see one or two Arctic convoy experiences as more of a whole will help us in the task of evaluating a part of this whole experience.

The chief thing to notice about these later convoys is the heavy battery of escorts that sailed with them. JW-61 left Loch Ewe on 20 October 1944. There were twenty-seven merchant vessels, a rescue ship, *Syrian Prince*, a Norwegian tanker, *Noreg*, and an oiler, *Laurelwood*. There was the 17th Destroyer Flotilla, with seven destroyers and the cruiser *Dido*. There were three carriers, *Vindex* (flagship of Admiral Dalrymple-Hamilton), *Nairana* and *Tracker*. This was a total, deep escort capability, which speaks volumes about the type of opposition anticipated.

The carriers occupied the rear central column of the convoy, so that they would steer into the wind for landing flights of their aircraft without disrupting the formation of ships in front of them.

The cruiser *Dido* had two functions, to co-operate with the destroyers in the event of enemy surface attack (hardly ever to be realised, but always to be prepared for), and, importantly, with their AA capability, to cover the cruisers if He 111 torpedo-bombers broke through their own air defences. And then there was the considerable air power capability in this convoy. The joint complement of aircraft on the carriers was 23 Swordfish, 16 Wildcats and 11 Avengers. This hyperbolic display of air power on Russian convoy support all stemmed from that very basic Woolworths carrier, *Avenger*, which went to the bottom during one of the actions for Operation Torch.

So JW-61 was extremely well looked after. It had borrowed for this occasion from the Western Approaches 3rd and 8th Escort Group the destroyer HMS *Walker*, with the sloops *Lapwing* and *Lark* and the corvettes *Camellia*, *Oxlip* and *Rhododendron*.

The main ocean escort was made up of the carriers and the cruiser, with the 17th Destroyer Flotilla under Captain Browning in *Onslow*, with *Obedient*, *Offa*, *Opportune*, *Oribi* and *Orwell*. There were two more escort groups, the 15th (with the frigates *Inglis*, *Lawson*, *Loring*, *Louis*, *Mounsey* and *Narborough*), and the 21st (*Conn*, *Byron*, *Deane*, *Fitzroy*, *Redmill* and *Rupert*). On *Conn* was the Senior Officer Lieutenant Commander R. Hart.

Formidable though this sounds, this grand roll of names of ships and men, and aircraft, they faced a wolfpack, code-named Panther, of nineteen boats, fitted with the Schnorkel, allowing them to run trimmed-down to periscope depth on their diesel engines. They were also armed with the Gnat, the T-5 acoustic torpedo.

Asdic operations in the Arctic

There had been some discussion at Western Approaches Command about the effectiveness of Asdic operations in the Barents Sea and Arctic waters. Temperatures and oceanic conditions in the Arctic produced fainter Asdic signals and echoes, what was called a 'layering' effect. North Atlantic waters were more homogeneous and more congenial to Asdic work, with a greater clarity and sharpness of signals. Lieutenant Commander Mosse was a zealot for the use of Asdic in the Arctic theatre. His efforts in HMS *Mermaid* were responsible for the death of two U-boats, one on his escorting of convoy JW-59 and one on escorting convoy RA-59A; and he reported to Captain Howard-Johnston, Director of the Anti-U-boat Division of Western Approaches that, though there was a tendency towards fainter Asdic echoes in Arctic operating conditions, nevertheless it could be done. Mosse backed up his well-chosen words with a typed, well-argued technical report.

Undoubtedly Mosse's intervention saved the day, and frustrated those members of Naval Staff, Western Approaches who said that anti-submarine work in support of Arctic convoys was an utter waste of time 'because they never had any hope of getting results with the Asdic'. Mosse's presence was vital, as well as his written report; for here was a man who had killed two U-boats on Arctic convoys. You could, he argued, kill U-boats operating in the Arctic, if you had well-trained and experienced Asdic operators in an anti-submarine team, 'though extra concentration was needed'.

Perhaps Mosse's intention at this time was chiefly remembered among all the top brass of Western Approaches by the astonishing, and, in questionable taste though it was, demonstrative visual aid he carried around with him.

Max Horton and a macabre trophy

Before talking to Howard-Johnston, both Mosse and Stannard (Lieutenant Commander R.B. Stannard VC, captain of *Peacock*) had to report to the Commander in Chief of Western Approaches, Admiral Max Horton, whereupon Mosse delivered to him a glass jar containing those mortal remains identified by *Peacock*'s naval surgeon as 'being of blood group four'. Horton shuddered, dedicated U-boat killers though he and 'Johnnie' Walker were, and this piece of Grand Guignol, gruesome though it was, achieved a kind of legendary status at Western Approaches.

There was appalling weather at the outset for convoy JW-61, which made the carriers pitch and roll heavily in the gale-force winds. During this weather it was difficult for a Swordfish to take off and land, when a Swordfish had an airspeed of no more than 30 knots.

Huff-Duff (HF/DF – High Frequency Direction Finder) operators picked up talk and other signals from U-boats. *Tracker* flew off two Avengers and two Wildcats, already in a state of instant readiness. An attack was made on the only U-boat they saw, which skilfully avoided the acoustic depth-charge that was dropped.

For two whole days, 26 and 27 October, the U-boats attacked the frigates in the allied escorts with their T-5 acoustic torpedoes, but the frigates foiled them with their 'foxers', those noisy devices trailing in the wake of the ship which diverted the acoustic torpedo from its true target, or with something called a 'step-aside procedure', which amounted to frequent alterations of course and speed.

Such a massive escort, in the end, failed to sink any U-boats. However, the convoy made its way to the Kola inlet, without losses, arriving on 28 October, while Russian destroyers took those who were berthing at Archangel on further to the White Sea. An unusual bonus for ships and crews waiting after the delivery of this convoy was a moving performance by a Russian choir on the hangar deck of the carrier HMS *Tracker*. This was superb. 'Why couldn't this be done more often?' men said.

RA-65

RA-65, the return convoy, saw thirty-seven ships return without loss to Loch Ewe on 9 November, having sailed on 2 November. There was one exception, the frigate HMS *Mounsey*, which was torpedoed by *U-295* with a T-5 acoustic torpedo. The ship had to return to the Kola inlet for repair. The escorts also lamented that they had not sunk a U-boat, and blamed what they called the poor Asdic conditions. They could not be persuaded that Asdic would work in the Arctic, maintaining their earlier opinion relentlessly, in the teeth of every kind of evidence to the contrary.

Collaborators' convoy: JW-61A

There was, however, one convoy which did not carry material for the Russian war effort. A small, unusual and, in the eyes of many, questionable convoy sailed from Liverpool to Murmansk on 31 October 1944. This convoy is part of the story, as it was part of Stalin's paranoia about allied treatment of Russian POWs. It was codenamed JW-61A and consisted of *Empress of Australia*, a Canadian Pacific liner, and *Scythia*, a Cunard ship. Both carried 11,000 'Russian Collaborators', as Stalin called them, most of them Ukrainians, and nearly all of them captured wearing Wehrmacht uniform, and fighting for the Germans in Norway.

Their 'repatriation' on arrival at Murmansk on 6 November was carefully handled by the Soviet authorities. The crews of the two liners and the British guards who accompanied the Ukrainians were not allowed to land. The last they saw of them was when they were marched off briskly into further prolonged and final captivity. The gulags of Stalin worked their inmates to death or, at any rate, with varying degrees of harshness, and the stigma of being a collaborator was one deserving of the highest penalty. It is likely that a proportion of them would have been shot anyway.

These transported collaborators did not want to go back to Russia, and a measure of force had to be applied, causing a number of the British soldiers who had the task of getting them in the ships and guarding them to become very upset indeed. But Stalin had insisted that they be repatriated to the USSR, and Churchill had just returned from what he described as a 'cordial' dialogue with Stalin, and wanted to maintain this relationship.

The liners were properly escorted by eight destroyers, and the frigates *Duckworth*, *Berry*, *Cooke*, *Domett*, *Essington* and *Rowley*, saw the return convoy RA-61 back home also, a convoy which caused much discussion and manifest deploring on the allied side. It was a piece of diplomatic amorality, and this convoy, together with numerous other such 'repatriations' have formed the subject of books and lawsuits, and caused much wringing of hands. It must be seen in the same spirit of mistrust that characterised the relationship between the allies and the USSR throughout the entire period of the Russian convoys, and which Brundle and other merchant seamen lamented.

Not long after the homeward convoy, RA-61, had returned to the UK after those odious repatriations, twenty-eight Lancaster bombers (which had flown from Lossiemouth to bases in Russia) succeeded in hitting *Tirpitz* in Tromso fiord in Norway, and capsizing her, with a loss of 1,000 of her crew.

Tirpitz and her end

The story of the final end of *Tirpitz* is one of dogged persistence, with a motto of 'If at first you don't succeed, try, try, try again'. Most of the aggressive operations carried out by the Kriegsmarine were carried out by U-boats. Hitler, much to the frustration of many senior officers, including Grossadmiral Raeder, kept the country's surface vessels cooped up and reined in. *Tirpitz* was always a threat to the Russian convoys. She was a 'sword of Damocles'. She had only to make a single aggressive sortie to obliterate a convoy. That, together with a failure in intelligence, was the psychology behind the fateful scattering of the PQ-17 convoy.

For seven months, January to July 1942, *Tirpitz* languished near Trondheim. On 5 July she left Trondheim for Altenfiord, but never closed with PQ-17, despite the infamous 'scatter' signal.

Back in Altenfiord until late October, she returned to Trondheim for a refit, which lasted until March 1943. Then it was back to Altenfiord. After that, *Tirpitz* only came out on the offensive once, when she joined the attack on a small British and Norwegian meteorological station at Spitzbergen on 6 September 1943. From January 1942 to October 1944 *Tirpitz* never fired at another warship or at any kind of vessel. Her sea time averaged two days per month. She remained there in the fiord, swinging from a buoy, with morale and training potential becoming more and more eroded.

In March and April 1942 Halifax bombers of 4 Group, Bomber Command, flying from Yorkshire bases, had been sent three times to bomb *Tirpitz*. There were problems of finding the ship in such a narrow and mountainous fiord, of the heavy barrage which scythed away bombers relentlessly, of an intense but tellingly effective smokescreen – and though the bombers and their crews, brave as lions, tried three times, twelve Halifaxes in all were lost, with most of the crews.

In October 1942 another attempt was made on *Tirpitz* using two-man human torpedoes. This too was a failure, chiefly because the two 'chariots', as they were called, which were slung under a fishing boat, broke lose in bad weather quite near to the target. For their desperately hazardous contribution Lieutenants Cameron and Place were each awarded the VC, even while they were still POWs.

Tirpitz may not have been destroyed but she was out of action for several months.

As for air attacks on *Tirpitz*, there were twenty-two of them. On 3 April 1944 there came a Fleet Air Arm attack, with Fairey Barracudas for torpedo attack and dive-bombing, and Grumman Wildcats and Hellcats for fighter cover. No significant strikes were made on *Tirpitz*, but she was put out of action for three months. The commanding officer of *Tirpitz* was wounded in this attack.

It was now the turn of 617 Squadron of Royal Air Force, Bomber Command. No. 617, the 'Dambusters' squadron were given the task of putting *Tirpitz* out of action with their Lancasters. But the return trip from Norway to the UK would be more than 3,000 miles. So how was it to be done?

In the end the Group Commander of 5 Group, AVM the Honourable Ralph Cochrane, decided that the attack could be conducted from a base within the Soviet Union, using an airfield at Yagodnik, which was an island in the Dvina River. This was 20 miles from Archangel, and just about 600 miles from Altenfiord, where *Tirpitz* lay.

The date for the final RAF raid of this series, after a number of visits, was set for 12 November. To save weight, now that they were carrying extra fuel tanks, there were to be no mid-upper gunners. The Lancasters took off in the early hours of

12 November. Flying at 1,000 feet above the sea, they were below the German radar.

When they reached Tromso the AA gunners of *Tirpitz* opened up. Smoke could have been expected, but was not forthcoming. The smoke pots had only just been moved down from Altenfiord, and the German defenders on *Tirpitz* had not yet primed and prepared them. During this RAF attack *Tirpitz* began to list. Meanwhile, happily for the attacking aircraft, there was no sign of fighters.

On the return journey bad weather effectively closed Lossiemouth. Tait, the commander of the strike, had to land at a smaller airfield nearby. When he eventually arrived at Lossiemouth, a Norwegian agent had confirmed that *Tirpitz* had capsized, with the loss of 1,204 members of the crew.

The Germans, after this reverse, turned to the interdiction of the convoys to Russia with a new fury and earnestness.

It was an undignified and inevitable end for Germany's chief battleship, the capital ship the mere hint of whose presence was sufficient to bring about the rerouting of populous convoys or even, in one infamous decision, the scattering of a convoy. The presence of *Tirpitz* and other powerful German surface vessels was the reason why Russian convoys had such powerful escorts. Air attack and U-boats could be expected, but it was the menace of those big grey ghosts coming over the horizon from the Norwegian fiords, imparting their threat of decimating a convoy, which loomed large (larger in the event than it should have done) in all operational planning in the convoy war.

U-boat crews: 'There are no roses on a sailor's grave'

To capsize *Tirpitz* like this certainly brought the means of victory nearer. But it was back in late 1943, with the sinking of *Scharnhorst*, that the balance of winning the Arctic campaign had begun to tip in favour of the allies. For, to look at the other side, and leaving aside German surface vessels for the moment, German U-boat losses were truly appalling. Dönitz's two sons died. If you go to Cuxhaven–Altenbruch, you will find a U-boat archive, invaluable to researchers. Very close to the archive is a memorial, vast and bleak, on which the names of all the U-boat men who died are carved. There are no war cemeteries, there cannot be for the one in four merchantmen lost at sea, or for all those U-boat men who fought to sink them. As the German poem for those killed at sea puts it, 'There are no roses on a sailor's grave'.

JW-62

The next convoy to North Russia, JW-62, after the demise of *Tirpitz*, sailed from Loch Ewe on 29 November 1944, without this sword of Damocles, the threat from the German surface fleet hanging over it. There were thirty merchant vessels, heavily escorted, with destroyers of the 8th Escort Group, with corvettes, sloops and frigates, with the 17th Destroyer Flotilla and the Canadian 9th Escort Group. Captain Ullring of the Royal Norwegian Navy was Commodore, while Rear Admiral McGrigor hoisted his flag in a carrier, HMS *Campania*, and there was another carrier present among the escorts, HMS *Nairana*, together with a cruiser, HMS *Bellona*.

Two wolfpacks of U-boats failed to harm any of the convoy, though patrol ships of the Soviet Northern Fleet succeeded in keeping away the most determined of U-boats, so that all the convoy reached Kildin Island without loss, some going to Murmansk, and others, two days later, in a White Sea contingent, to Archangel.

The U-boats were making an all-out stand against the convoys. Withdrawn from the Atlantic, the U-boats' only important quarry was the convoys to Russia. The fact that convoys up to the end of the war were vigorously and mightily escorted with powerful vessels of considerable firepower, and most times with an air component (consider the two carriers on JW-62), speaks a lot about the importance of the Russian run as a dangerous and significant theatre of war, one which challenged the allies to the extreme and exacted a quota of casualties to the very end.

Admiral Sir Andrew Cunningham, the First Sea Lord, at the end of 1944, expressed concern at the casualties the newly refurbished enemy submarines were causing. The Schnorkel on the Type VII and XI boats had given U-boats the facility to move independently without surfacing, while the Gnat was making inroads on the convoys, let alone the appearance of the vastly superior type XXI and XXIII U-boats.

It is no exaggeration to say that these new challenges had to be met, or the allies would suffer an untimely reverse in the war at sea, which might jeopardise a peace and the movement towards a German surrender.

Sinking of HMS *Bluebell* and HMS *Goodall*

Casualties were being sustained by the allies until the very end. On 17 February 1945 the corvette HMS *Bluebell*, one of the escorts in convoy RA-64, blew up after a torpedo attack, and the entire crew, with the exception of one man, perished.

The very last casualty in the Russian convoys and, indeed, in the European theatre, was the torpedoing of the American-built Captain Class frigate HMS *Goodall* on 29 April 1945 in convoy RA-66. However, in the same convoy two U-boats were sunk. Despite the courage of the captain of HMS *Honeysuckle*, who ran alongside *Goodall* to take off her crew, the ship exploded and damaged the corvette, sinking with heavy loss of life.

No rest for the convoy men

The allied seamen on their convoys were never able to relax. Constant vigilance was required at all times. Contrast this situation with that faced by the U-boat crews.

The Schnorkel solved the problem of U-boat vulnerability on the surface. The diesel engines running underwater meant that the boats could travel much faster when they were submerged than was possible with electric motor power. The diesel engines, furthermore, could recharge the U-boat's batteries underwater. But there was a dark side to life in a U-boat crew. At this stage of the war, with such a fearsome attrition rate for crews, about 50 per cent of U-boat crews at sea were on their first voyage. Furthermore, the fact that the Schnorkel-equipped U-boats seldom resurfaced meant that some of those among the young crews were visited by appalling seasickness, and a creeping claustrophobia, known to those in U-boats as *Blechkrankheit*, 'tin-can-itis', an aversion to living in a tin can, and to living out of tin cans.

To the allies and to allied seamen there was an unpredictability about the U-boats, even after Dönitz, on 4 May, had instructed his U-boat captains to cease from hostile actions. All U-boats in the Arctic and North Atlantic were instructed to move to Loch Eriboll (south of the Orkneys and on the Scottish mainland) to surrender.

There were, however, still many convinced, and even fanatical, Nazis among U-boat crews. That was why it was decided to continue the convoys for several weeks after the official end of hostilities. It was a salutary thought that a dozen or so of the new type XXI U-boats were already in commission, with many, many more in a process of working up, or undergoing trials and crew training.

RA-67

While many U-boats were surrendering and making for, or being escorted to, Loch Eriboll, the last convoy to leave Russia, RA-67, arrived in the estuary of the Clyde on 30 May 1945. There was, of course, a significant difference between this and previous convoys. Every ship had her navigation lights blazing, and the shore of Gourock and Greenock was an explosion of lights too.

Robert Brundle on Atlantic and Mediterranean convoys

These heavily escorted final few convoys to Russia grew out of those early convoys of 1941 and early 1942, of eight or ten ships, with an escort of half that number, five warships (two minesweepers, two destroyers and a light cruiser). The heavy, deep escorts grew out of this early, simple pattern, when the need was to get everything through to Murmansk or Archangel, all the ships, all the cargoes, to succour a Russia under siege at Moscow and Leningrad. From that moment onwards, however, it became an indelible part of allied strategy, and of allied provision for Russia, with the tide of war turning from a Russia under siege to a Russia advancing victoriously, in the wake of Stalingrad and Kursk. After such ruinous but victorious battles Russia had all the more need for new and improved American tanks. The shortest means of equipping their ally with American tanks was via the North route to Russia.

Brundle, by contrast, in his last few convoys, was sailing in other waters, different oceans. In his last few convoys he had a spell in the Mediterranean: a convoy to Gibraltar, and then from Liverpool to Freetown, Sierra Leone and back, and finally in January 1945 a convoy, again from Liverpool, to Marseilles and then Oran.

He had sailed, even before the war, to every major port in the world. Prior to the North Russian experience he had had a spell on Atlantic convoys and had seen sinkings and the activities of the U-boat scourge. He had come ashore at Halifax, Nova Scotia, where families were warm and hospitable to merchant seamen, and New York, which, with its blaze of lights and razzamatazz, was unforgettable. But then he had known New York as a young Second Officer and Chief Officer in an earlier war. Convoys to Gibraltar were often harassed by U-boats and the inevitable spotter planes. He had one bad Gibraltar convoy, but nothing on the scale of Murmansk and North Russia. To borrow the phrase from Apsley Cherry-Garrard, an Antarctic explorer on the Scott expedition, who wrote a book of that title, that was the 'Worst Journey in the World'.

It was not just the extreme weather conditions, not the U-boats, nor the air attacks, even though he had experienced all three. It was the sight of men from a doomed ship in the water, frozen stiff after two minutes, and almost glad to welcome death when it came. It was the sight of hungry people, particularly women and children, tubercular and shivering, begging on the quays of Murmansk. It was the appalling waste of those ships blown up at their berths, with their cargo undischarged, with their DEMS gunners blazing away at those low-level Ju 88s during one of the almost daily Murmansk air raids, until they, like the rest of their crews, were overwhelmed by the tearing, coruscating explosion that killed the ship and the men on its decks, and which could so easily have been the fate of *Harmatris* and her crew. It was the desperate fate he saw, on the journey of QP-14, overtaking all those ships, *Leda* and *Silver Sword*, *Somali*, with, at length, her broken back and the loss of life occasioned by that final sinking; *Bellingham*, *Ocean Voice*, and that unglamorous maid of all work, the fleet oiler *Gray Ranger*, spilling out her oil for her crew to become clogged and decimated and trapped in, for oil can sustain or kill. It was the sight and speech of the two shipless captains in Archangel, Captain Stephenson of *Hartlebury* and Captain Wharton of *Empire Byron*, who lamented their ships and their lost crews, swallowed up by PQ-17, and who, knowing something of the fellowship of the sea, and of the loneliness of command, cordially wished him well, and a safe passage in QP-14. Seamen look one another in the eye when they say these things. They are a combination of toughness and sentimentality. They wear hardship like a second skin, but they can and do melt. These things plucked at his heart strings, and moved him more than most other things.

For one thing there were so many unspoken goodbyes in that terrible period. Captain Stephenson, for one, ill and with a shocking wound in his head, died after that final meeting, the only master of a ship to perish of the 153 seamen who went down from the convoy PQ-17.

As Brundle turned to face the challenges of peacetime, the convoy experience, all that pride and hope, all that grief and waste, was dinning in his head. Four hundred years ago Thomas Traherne, an English mystic, wrote: 'You never enjoy the world aright, till the sea itself floweth in your veins.' Brundle had had his joy of the sea, and it was time for him to find out whether something else might flow in his veins, time for him (long overdue) to 'enjoy the world aright'.

CHAPTER 9

'Home is the Sailor'

Under the wide and starry sky,
Dig the grave and let me lie.
Glad did I live and gladly die,
And I laid me down with a will.
This be the verse you grave for me:
Here he lies where he longed to be,
Home is the sailor, home from the sea,
And the hunter home from the hill.

Robert Louis Stevenson
'Requiem' from *Underwoods*, 1887

The Corfu Incident: mined off Albania

The Russian convoys were not my grandfather's only brush with death and danger. 'Bob Brundle always seems to go where things happen', one friend and colleague said. On 1 January 1947 the ship he was then Master of, *Harberton* (another J. & C. Harrison ship, like *Harmatris*, which he commanded during the war), struck a mine in the narrow channel between Corfu (which was part of Greece) and Albania. The ship struck the mine at 11.30pm on 1 January 1947 and major damage was done. A young rating, Joe Foster, from South Shields, was on lookout in the bow of the ship, and was killed, a sadness to the rest of the crew, and a great grief to his family. Somehow this was something not looked for or expected in peacetime. Brundle was wounded in the explosion, sustaining injury to his legs.

HMS *Mermaid* came to the assistance of *Harberton*, with several Greek tugs, towing her to Piraeus, the port of Athens, for necessary and summary repairs, something accomplished with dispatch (contrast the long and weary Murmansk experience). *Mermaid* was the ship written about in the previous chapter, which was an escort in JW-59, commanded, in wartime, by the redoubtable Lieutenant Commander Mosse, who destroyed two U-boats while acting as her commander.

Albania, which was responsible for laying the mines off her coastline, and in the Corfu channel, had become a political and social pariah to western governments and to the United Nations ever since the coming to power of the hard-line Stalinist regime of Enver Hoxha, who headed a brutal anti-western government for forty years.

In the recent war Britain had supplied agents, via the SOE organisation, who had parachuted into Albania to help the resistance against the Germans. After the Germans withdrew, a brief civil war ensued, and brave and legendary SOE operatives, like Julian Amery (son of Leo Amery, and brother of the ill-starred John Amery, executed for treason), David Smiley, and 'Billy' McLean were chagrined at all the sacrifices of courageous colleagues and partisans having resulted in this.

In October 1946 two British destroyers, HMS *Saumarez* and HMS *Volage*, were the first ships to strike mines in the Corfu channel, and forty-three British sailors were killed. The experience of Brundle in *Harberton* was the last incident of this kind. They were fortunate that more lives were not lost, but a life is a life, and there was a little knot of South Shielders on board who knew Joe Foster, and whose families lived near his. Brundle and the ship's crew were enormously saddened by the incident. The crew were family, and, as already said, after the wartime experience, this sort of tragedy was totally unexpected, and a great shock to all.

Diplomatic links between Britain and Albania were already bad, and were now severed, after Britain accused Albania of deliberately sowing mines in the Corfu channel. One factor that aggravated the international aspect of things was that Albania was enigmatically aiding and giving sanctuary to the Communist side in the Greek Civil War, which was then raging. Indeed, before Enver Hoxha took over there had been a small civil war between the supporters of the former King Zog and Hoxha's hard-line Stalinist partisans. Britain was awarded damages for all incidents relating to the Corfu channel by the International Court in The Hague. Albania refused to pay these damages. In retaliation and as a reprisal Britain held on to a quantity of gold belonging to Albania, which had been deposited in the Bank of England for safekeeping during the war.

Sir Winston Churchill wrote about the incident in terms of strong condemnation, holding that:

> It is not a matter which can be ignored or forgotten because it occurred in time of peace, and cannot be ... swept into the confused catalogue of human injuries and wrong desires which were done on both sides in the course of the great war.

Later he wrote, 'Not the slightest satisfaction has been obtained for the outrage of ingratitude and treachery.'

Brundle's thoughts, as he reflected on his ship's involvement in sustaining the final casualty in what the diplomats and international experts called the Corfu Incident, must have often gone back to Murmansk and Archangel and the appalling background of the Russian convoys.

He had plenty of time to make such reflections, as the year after the Albanian mining incident he retired from seafaring and from working for J. & C. Harrison. Looking at those subsequent convoys, after PQ-8, and including QP-14, it emerges that the entire *raison d'être* of those sailing on the convoy was to 'fight the convoy through, to expect trouble and to deal with it', and Brundle's journey on *Harmatris*, from fire to U-boat attack, to leaving and re-boarding the ship that would not sink, from air attack to eight months in Murmansk and Archangel, contained trouble enough and to spare.

To 'fight the convoy through'

This was the business of the escort vessels of the Royal Navy throughout the period of the Russian convoys and they carried this out to the letter at the cost of 18 warships (of which HMS *Matabele* was the first) and the lives of 1,944 sailors. Turning to those merchant vessels they protected with their lives, 87 ships were lost, at a cost of 829 lives of allied merchant seamen.

Considering the suspicions entertained by the Russians which issued in the Cold War of the post-war period (of which the Corfu Incident was part), the Arctic run was the most amazing example of co-operation between allied governments. My grandfather was a great admirer of the achievements, bought with much suffering, of the Red Army, and the thought of what they were doing sustained him during the hard times of the convoys. But his Russian experiences in Murmansk and Archangel and the complete absence of compassion and co-operation shown to sailors in Russian ports, unwinding after the taut twilight world of the Arctic convoys, chilled him to the bone, and brought him massive disillusionment.

In March 1943 he was asked a question when he was summoned to the Admiralty to make his report. 'And what do you think of our Russian allies, Brundle?' 'I'd have to stand up in Trafalgar Square and whisper it, Sir', he replied.

Awards and decorations

PQ-8 and the story of *Harmatris* became known through the award of medals and decorations. Captain R.W. Brundle, of Driffield, Yorkshire was awarded the OBE, and the Lloyd's War Medal.

The Chief Engineering Officer, Mr William Kelly Surtees Robinson, of Sunderland, and the Chief Officer, Mr George Edwin Masterman, of West Hartlepool, were each awarded the MBE, and the Chief Steward, Mr Ronald Peart, of Barry, Glamorgan, who helped to fight the fire, was awarded the BEM. These awards were gazetted on 16 March 1943.

All these recipients of awards were from the ship's company of *Harmatris*. The representatives of the owners, who were present at the Admiralty interview Robert Brundle had in 1943, noticed, 'with great pleasure' in a letter to him the honour conferred on him by HM The King, and expressed the satisfaction of their Company 'that your services have been so recognised'.

The story of PQ-8 and the saga of *Harmatris* was widely reported in the national press from March 1943 onwards. There were a number of similar stories connected with the Atlantic convoys and Malta convoys as well as with the Russian convoys doing the rounds, and the public were avid for news of Merchant Navy personnel and their doings.

Harmatris and her story was an early example from the Russian convoys, although, due to the eight months in Murmansk and Archangel the awards were not gazetted until March 1943. *The Daily Mail*, *The Daily Telegraph*, the Merchant Navy *Neptune* magazine and the Cunard magazine, *The Syren and Shipping*, among others, had a full report. Captain Schofield of the Trades Division of the Admiralty and the owners of *Harmatris*, J. & C. Harrison, gave their seal of approval to this. Let us return to the convoys themselves.

An unsound principle of war

'A fundamentally unsound principle of war', Admiral Tovey called the Russian convoys, when Churchill made his promise to Stalin in 1941. And yet the first few Russian convoys passed with no fatalities although PQ-6 was worried and harassed. PQ-8 was a watershed, the first Arctic convoy to be 'bloodied', trailing signals that the Germans were now in earnest, and bringing in its train evidence of perseverance, resilience and dogged stubbornness in the face of everything the weather and the war could throw at *Harmatris*: fire amidships, three torpedoes, a refusal to abandon ship while she still floated, two boardings and re-boardings, air attacks while under towing for the Kola inlet, eight months in Murmansk and Archangel being bombed perpetually before a journey home on QP-14 through a cordon of U-boats, which sank some escorts and merchant ships. Master and crew all arrived safely home, although Captain Brundle wrote in his report that it was 'the most disappointing voyage of my career'.

The contribution of the Russian convoys

Afterwards in the years of the Cold War western military historians argued that the motives behind the Russian convoys were almost entirely political, and that what was sent did not reflect the real needs of the Russian fighting machine. And yet the physical reality of the tanks, fuel, ammunition and locomotives was a real and ever-present help which gave the Red Army the marrow and sinews of resistance until the tide turned at Stalingrad. Murmansk was important enough to have diverted to obliterate it entire swathes of German aircraft. And Murmansk was important enough for convoy crews to give and endure everything to get there with their vital cargoes. It was important to keep Murmansk, the entry port for the allied convoys, free and in Russian hands, as the only ice-free port in the region, a port of refuge and resort in the unremittingly bleak weather.

Two minutes in the Arctic waters around the Kola inlet were enough to bring death to sailors whose ships had been sunk. Sailors from HMS *Matabele* suffered such a death in the outgoing convoy PQ-8, and sailors in HMS *Leda* and *Somali* (like *Matabele* a Tribal Class destroyer) suffered in the return convoy QP-14, in which *Harmatris* returned home.

Murmansk was of vital strategic importance, and, quite apart from all the freight for the Soviet army the allied ships brought with them, their actions kept Murmansk free. From Murmansk there was a railway to Moscow, and Murmansk was near the besieged city of Leningrad, invested by the Germans for 900 days, at a cost of the lives of over a million of its inhabitants. To the merchantmen and Royal Navy sailors in these bombed-out ports there was no doubt of the supreme importance of what they were doing, whatever the hostile reception of the official representatives.

The story of PQ-8 contains many of the elements of later convoys more populous in ships, more heavily escorted. It is a tale of a small convoy in the early months of the Arctic convoys' progress, which exemplifies the principle that the convoy, any convoy, large or small, and its cargo must go through.

Russian ingratitude

And Russian ingratitude? Well, gratitude was never an easy virtue, and as so often, in numerous other circumstances Churchill had a story for it, which illustrates Russian ingratitude and runs as follows:

> *A little boy fell into Portsmouth dock, and would have drowned, had it not been for the vigilance and alacrity of a passing Jack Tar in his tiddley suit, who dived in and rescued him.*
>
> *The next day the boy with his mother were out on the dock going for a walk. The heroic sailor, who had risked his life in the oily, dirty water of the dock, only the day before, just then passed the boy and his mother out on their walk. Tugging excitedly on his mother's sleeve, the boy said, 'That's the man who pulled me out of the water yesterday, mummy!'. Turning to the sailor, the mother asked 'Are you the man who pulled Derek out of the water?' 'Yes, maam,' replied the matelot, standing to a mock, polite attention, and expecting, if not to be rewarded, at least to be thanked for his pains. But, fixing her eyes on the poor serviceman, with mounting anger the mother cried out 'Then, what have you done with his cap?'*

Truth and truism: myth and fact

Such humour, like many kinds of laughter, acknowledges the tears of things, and can on occasions chill the heart. When we contemplate such suffering, such painful endurance, such simple heroism and such desolating loss that characterises the tale of the Russian convoys we must be humble, offering our hearts and opening our fountains of sympathy to those for whom the convoys are for ever an ineluctable symbol of loss. 'That was where my boy went down', someone said to me, 'swallowed up for ever by the Arctic Ocean.'

Churchill's story of the boy at the dock is a truism, which means it is a story containing truths, and at the same time, elements beyond truth, that is, elements that reflect the truth of the situation, set alongside elements that make a myth out of all Russian convoy situations. Here is another story, a true story this time. Not that a myth is untrue, much less a lie. It is just that all myths, all truisms depend on a number of basic truths and facts to make them up, to give to these myths substance and standing.

So here, then, is this true story about a poet, and his lost friend.

Charles Causley, the sailor poet, and a lost friend

The Cornish poet Charles Causley, who served in the Royal Navy during the war, used, after the war, to pass every day on his way to work at Launceston a woman who had lost her son in one of the Russian convoys. This boy was his school friend and left Launceston with him for the Navy at the same time as he did in 1940, and had perished. As Causley passed the woman each day (who always had a look of 'Why my boy and not you?') he reflected, 'I found myself haunted by the words in the twenty-fourth chapter of St Matthew: 'Then shall two be in the field; the one shall be taken, and the other left.''

So Causley put his feelings into his poetry, and I fancy that one of the poems he wrote is a commemoration, among others, of his departed friend from Launceston. The poem is addressed to the boy's mother, the mother whom Causley encountered weekday after weekday for most of the rest of her life in the streets of Launceston: It is called 'Song of the Dying Gunner AA1', and envisages a naval ack-ack (or anti-aircraft) gunner, who, let us say, has been struck by a bullet sprayed in one of those low-level attacks by a Ju 88 or an He 111, just as the merchant ship (when he would be one of the DEMS gunners) or the destroyer was approaching the Kola inlet:

> Oh Mother my mouth is full of stars
> As cartridges in the tray
> My blood is a twin-branched scarlet tree
> And it runs all runs away.
>
> Oh 'Cooks in the galley' is sounded off
> And the lads are down in the mess
> But I lie done by the forrard gun
> With a bullet in my breast.

Don't send me a parcel at Christmas time
of socks and nutty and wine
And don't depend on a long weekend
by the Great Western Railway line.

Farewell Aggie Weston, the barracks at Guz,
Hang my tiddley suit on the door.
I'm sewn up neat in a canvas sheet
And I shan't be home no more.

Perhaps Causley's friend went down in HMS *Matabele*, when an entire ship's company but two were wiped out! Deeply troubling, deeply shocking, like the earlier disaster, to a whole nation, of the demise of *Hood*. Deeply troubling, both for the two survivors and the men who sailed in the other escorts and merchantmen, and deeply troubling for those who sent them out. Deeply troubling most of all for the lady at Launceston, the bereaved mother, who reminded Charles Causley of the human cost. For everyone was some mother's son. Everyone represented, stood for an ocean of heartache, a lifetime of grieving. Life, any life lost violently in war, is never lost lightly.

Memories and memorabilia

My family knew this at the time of my father's death in Bomber Command in April 1944. Thereafter Robert Brundle played a part, together with my paternal grandfather, Tom Wadsworth, good grandfathers, both of them twin pillars of being the significant male presence in my life and upbringing.

That is why it has been so hard not to have been able to ask my grandfather, Robert Brundle, about the Russian run and Murmansk. He died when I was 17. There was just that God-forsaken garden shed, now having yielded its territory to a building plot, and those American sheets, which were saved, along with other useful flotsam and jetsam, from sliding eventually into Murmansk harbour, and which I almost wore down to a thread. Thank you, Uncle Sam.

And yet there are the reports my grandfather wrote, in which I can hear his voice, economic and matter of fact, speaking through the photographs of a damaged and shattered ship, and the things people wrote about him and *Harmatris* in newspapers and magazines. These remain, and have fed this narrative. And also, yes, the chair, the chair he was given from the captain's cabin of *Harmatris*, the chair he sat on, the chair which takes me on his journey, the chair which takes me further on, as his life ended at the same age as my own current age, but for a few months. I am sitting on this chair now. I have written this account sitting on it. I sit on it a lot, and I muse and I mend.

'Home is the sailor'

Robert Brundle was an ordinary man, of absolutely no pretensions, gifted with humour, however, but with a brow 'like Mars to threaten and command', to quote Shakespeare, and with uncommon Yorkshire stubbornness.

In the last years he had his eyes fixed as if on some distant horizon. And yet he had a lovely smile, and by his constant singing at home he used to bring something of the Edwardian Music Hall to my life. I shall not easily forget his rendering of 'When father papered the parlour, you couldn't see him for paste', or of that haunting ragtime number 'Won't you come home, Bill Bailey, won't you come home?', a kind of paradigm of his seafaring life. Bill Bailey, a name beloved of today's stand-up comedians, was, I've discovered in reality, one of those expatriate colonial chancers, hardy perennials, who just wouldn't, or, in the end, couldn't leave the louche, down-at-heel bar he ran in Singapore.

The distant look seemed to confirm that, unlike Bill Bailey, Robert Brundle knew he was coming home. His tombstone in Driffield cemetery, in a lovely spot, has on it those words from Robert Louis Stevenson: 'Home is the sailor.' I wish, as a boy and young man, I'd had more of him, but it has been a rare privilege and a great delight to walk in his footsteps, even to Murmansk, even to the 'land on the edge of the world', as the Laplanders called it in the Sami language.

Bibliography

Primary Sources

Details of convoys PQ-6 and PQ-8 are to be found in Captain R.W. Brundle's *Admiralty Reports*, embodied and included in documents held in The National Archives, Kew, as ADM 199/72 and ADM 237/160.

Details of convoy QP-14 are also to be found in Captain R.W. Brundle's Admiralty Reports, and in ADM 199/721, 757, 758 and 1709, and in ADM 237/177, also in The National Archives, Kew.

Non-Fiction

Patricia Aithie: *The Burning Ashes of Time* (Seren Books 2005)

Ewart Brookes: *The Gates of Hell* (Arrow 1973)

Clay Blair: *Hitler's U-boat War* (Vol I, *The Hunters, 1939–1942*); (Vol II *The Hunted, 1942–1945*) (Cassell and Co. 2000)

Bernard Edwards: *The Merchant Navy Goes to War* (Robert Hall 1990)

Bernard Edwards: *The Road to Russia* (Pen and Sword 2002)

David Irving: *The Destruction of Convoy PQ.17* (Corgi 1970)

Paul Kemp: *Convoy: Drama in Arctic Waters* (Cassell Military Paperbacks 1993)

Brian Lavery: *In Which They Served: The RN Officer Experience in the Second World War* (Conway 2008)

Tony Lane: *The Merchant Seaman's War* (Manchester University Press 1990)

P. Lund and H. Ludlam: *PQ17: Convoy to Hell* (New English Library 1970)

Martin Middlebrook: *Convoy: The Greatest U-boat Battle of the War* (Cassell Military Paperbacks 2004)

Nicholas Monsarrat: *Life is a Four Letter Word Volume II – Breaking Out* (Cassell 1970)

Hugh Sebag-Montefiore: *Enigma: The Battle for the Code* (Weidenfield and Nicholson 2000)

D.F. White: *Bitter Ocean* (Headline Review 2007)

Godfrey Winn: *PQ-17: A Story of a Ship* (Hutchinson 1953)

Godfrey Winn: *The Positive Hour* (Michael Joseph 1970)

R. Winney: *The U-boat Peril* (Cassell Military Paperbacks 1986)

Richard Woodman: *Arctic Convoys* (John Murray 1994)

Richard Woodman: *The Real Cruel Sea: The Merchant Navy in the Battle of the Atlantic* (John Murray 2005)

Richard Woodman: *The History of the Ship* (Conway Maritime Press 2005)

David Wragg: *Swordfish* (Cassell Military Paperbacks 2004)

David Wragg: *Sacrifice for Stalin* (Pen and Sword 2005)

Fiction

Per Hansson: *One in Ten Had to Die* (George Allen & Unwin Ltd 1970)

Robert Harris: *Enigma* (Arrow Books 1995)

Jan de Hartog: *The Captain* (New English Library 1967)

Alistair Maclean: *HMS Ulysses* (Collins Fontana 1960)

Nicholas Monsarrat: *The Cruel Sea* (Cassell 1951)

Glossary

Nautical Terms

AA:	Anti-aircraft (e.g. guns, ships etc.).
Abaft:	Behind, in relation to something on the ship.
Abeam:	At right angles to the fore and aft line of the ship.
Able Seaman:	Certified seaman.
Aft, After:	Towards the stern.
After deck:	That part of the maindeck abaft the bridge.
Aggie Weston:	A term used by sailors to describe the temperance hostels founded in many seaports by Dame Agnes Weston.
Airpipe:	Pipe leading from ballast or fuel tanks to deck through which air escapes.
Asdic:	Submarine detection gear based on subsonic transmission.
Astern:	Behind the ship.
Azimuth:	Compass-bearing of sun, stars, etc.
Ballast:	Heavy material (e.g. steel pipes or wooden posts or props) loaded onto an empty ship to improve the stability of the vessel and to stop it rolling, usually on the homeward run, after the cargo has been delivered.
Beam ends:	When a vessel rolls very heavily to one side or the other she is said to be 'on her beam ends'.

Bilge:	Channel at bottom of hold or engine-room into which sea water drains.
Boat Deck:	The deck on which lifeboats are stowed.
Boat stations:	Stand by on boat deck to abandon ship.
Boatswain:	Senior rating on deck.
Bulkhead:	Steel or wooden partition between a ship's compartments.
CAM Ship:	Catapult Aircraft Merchant Ship: A ship with a multi-rocket-powered catapult fitted over the forecastle, on which a Mark I Hurricane is made ready, and is (literally) catapulted into action. After the aircraft's sortie, the pilot baled out and hoped to be picked up by an escort within 3 minutes.
Captain/Master:	In command.
Captain/officers:	Ranks in Merchant Navy.
Chief officer/ First mate:	Senior deck officer. Responsible for maintenance of hull and decks. Usually in charge of bridge on 4 to 8 watch.
Second officer/ mate:	Navigating officer. Keeps 12 to 4 watch.
Third officer/ mate:	Signals officer. Keeps 8 to 12 watch.
Radio officer:	Operates and maintains wireless telegraphy equipment.
Chief engineer:	Senior engine-room officer. Responsible to Captain for smooth running of engines and auxiliary machinery.
Second engineer:	Responsible for maintenance of engines and auxiliary machinery. Usually keeps 4 to 8 watch in engine-room.
Third engineer:	Keeps 12 to 4 watch and is also responsible for electrical repairs.
Fourth engineer:	Keeps 8 to 12 watch in engine-room.
Fifth engineer:	Usually on day work in engine-room and on deck, as required.
Chief steward:	In charge of catering.
Degaussing:	A process (called after a German scientist, Gauss) to wipe ships clean and neutralise

	them against the effects of magnetic mines by passing an electrical cable around them in port before a voyage.
DEMS:	Defensively Equipped Merchant Ship. Initials used to identify Royal Navy and Royal Artillery ratings seconded to merchant ships to man and maintain guns.
Deck boy:	Seaman in training.
Donkeyman:	Senior engine-room rating.
Fireman:	Attends boiler furnaces.
Dog watch:	The 4 to 8pm watch is sometimes divided into two 'dog' watches. The first dog watch is 4 to 6pm, the second at 6 to 8pm.
Eight bells:	Struck to signal the change of watches, i.e. at midnight, 4am, 8am, noon, 4pm, 8pm.
Foxer:	A device trailing in the water behind British ships to decoy German T-5 acoustic torpedoes, homing in on the noise they made, and causing them to explode harmlessly away from the ship (see Gnat below).
Forecastle:	Crews' quarters at fore end of ship.
Forecastle head:	Raised deck at fore end of ship.
Fore deck:	That part of the main deck forward of the bridge.
Gnat:	Nickname for German T-5 acoustic torpedoes, used in a later phase of the war. 'Gnat' is an acronym for German naval acoustic torpedo, as well as a reference to the noise it made.
GRT:	Gross registered tonnage.
Gunwale:	The uppermost planking of an open boat.
Guz:	Naval slang for Devonport.
Hatchway:	Opening on deck giving access to hold.
Heave-to:	To stop the ship at sea.
HF/DF:	High Frequency Direction Finder, called 'Huff-Duff' by all who used it. Used to intercept enemy signals and plot the position of U-boats.

Jolly boat:	Small general-purpose rowing boat.
Ju 88:	German twin-engined bomber and torpedo-carrying aircraft.
Lascar:	Indian or Somali seaman.
Lighter:	Barge.
Main deck:	The principal deck on a vessel having several decks.
Middle watch:	Midnight to 4am, and noon to 4pm.
MOWT:	(Ministry of War Transport) – the body which took over the work of providing ships and crews from the Board of Trade during wartime. Worked closely with Sea Transport Organisation (q.v.).
NCSO:	(Naval Control of Shipping Officers) – the body, staffed by retired naval officers, which handled movement by ships in British and American ports on behalf of the Admiralty. Took up concerns of ships' Masters and made sure they had all they needed. Fielded complaints by ships' masters.
PO:	Petty Officer. Senior NCO on the lower decks of an RN ship.
CPO:	Chief Petty Officer.
Quartermaster:	Steers ship and keeps gangway watches in port.
SBNONR:	Senior British Naval Officer, North Russia. A senior naval officer, resident in one of the North Russia ports, in charge of all the allied personnel, and of their operations, on the sea and in the air. Usually of the rank of Admiral or Rear Admiral.
Schnorkel:	A device in a later make of U-boat which allowed the boat to stay underneath for long periods, without coming to the surface. With diesel engines running underwater the boats travel faster, submerged, much farther also than with the previous electric motors. Diesel engines, furthermore, could recharge the U-boat's batteries underwater.

Squid:	An anti-submarine mortar, which lobbed small depth-charges ahead of a vessel pursuing a U-boat. In the hands of an experienced practitioner could be very effective.
STO:	Sea Transport Organisation. A body which dealt with the procurement and requisitioning of merchant ships for purposes related to the war effort. This included the repair of ships and bringing them to a state of seaworthiness. Britain needed to charter hundreds of ships, both from neutral countries, and those flying flags of convenience (e.g. Panama, Honduras, Liberia).
Tiddley suit:	Sailor's best shore-going uniform with gold badges.
Trimmer:	Engine-room rating who supplies firemen with coal.
'Tweendeck:	First deck below the main deck.
Well deck:	Space on the main deck, either between the raised forecastle and the bridge or between the latter poop.
Windlass:	Steam or electric winch used for raising anchors.
W/T:	Wireless telegraphy.

Index

Sub-headings appear in approximate chronological order where appropriate.